early med

C000301904

be

ined

• • • ellipsis

early medieval europe

the informal contained

First published 2001 by

●●●ellipsis
2 Rufus Street
London
N1 6PE
EMAIL ...@ellipsis.co.uk
www http://www.ellipsis.com

ISBN 1 899858 52 0

Publisher Tom Neville
Designed by Jonathan Moberly
Layout and image processing by Heike Löwenstein
Drawings by John Hewitt
Glossary by Andrew Wyllie
Index by Diana LeCore
Printed and bound in Hong Kong

British Library Cataloguing in Publication Data: a catalogue
record for this publication is available from the British Library
For a copy of the Ellipsis catalogue or information on special
quantity orders of Ellipsis books please contact sales on
020 7739 3157 or sales@ellipsis.co.uk

contents

The 'Middle Ages' were defined by 15th-century Italian chroniclers to distinguish the period between the destruction of Greco-Roman civilisation by the northern barbarians and the rebirth of its humanist values in their time. Both positive and negative, the barbarian contribution was crucial, yet the basis for the political and spiritual life of that medieval era – and much beyond it – was laid in the late 3rd and early 4th centuries by two of the greatest Roman emperors, Diocletian and Constantine the Great.

Finding the empire beyond the control of one man, Diocletian (284–305) divided it into four prefectures within which the old provinces were replaced by 12 dioceses subdivided into new provinces. The civil and military powers of the proconsuls who had governed the old provinces were also split, the former between the 'vicars' and 'counts' of the new dioceses and provinces, the latter to generals responsible directly to the emperor. Diocletian assigned his prefectures to a tetrarchy of associate emperors. But after his demise

1 **Monk at study in a monastery (St Gregory the Theologian)** 12th-century manuscript illumination (St Catherine's Monastery, Mount Sinai).

the heir to one of these, Constantine (324–37), reasserted undivided authority over the empire and moved his seat east from Rome to the old Greek city of Byzantium, which he refounded as Constantinople.

Diocletian left an administration concerned primarily with taxation to pay for the army, the bureaucracy and the court. Constantine the Great, as he was to be called, reformed the currency and tax system to encourage enterprise and achieved economic revival, but after him the state prospered at the expense of its citizens: many were taxed out of land and industry, their assets passed to the imperial regime or its great magnates and they became serfs tied to the land of others. With state ownership of the means of production, distribution and supply went state organisation of labour – a caste system, tying each worker and his children to a particular profession. As any improvement of the individual lot was taxed at a still higher rate there was little incentive and many of the dispossessed sought solace in a kingdom that was not of this world: the kingdom of Christ.

Jesus of Nazareth, the 'chosen one' ('Christos' in Greek), began his mission to lead man back to God in the third decade of the era that bears his name. Hailed by his followers as the Messiah, the Saviour, the Son of God, he was crucified for blasphemy at the instigation of the Jewish hierarchy (see volume 4, IMPERIAL SPACE, page 124), but in the faith of his devotees he rose from the dead to join his Father in Heaven.[1]

Instituting his church for the salvation of the faithful, Christ entrusted his follower Peter with its construction. Outlawed by the Jewish establishment, that church was built abroad, in the world of Rome – where, as uncompromising in its commitment to the One True God as the Judaism from which it sprang, Christianity was bound eventually to clash with imperial paganism. Persecution was spasmodic during the first three centuries but under Diocletian the state found it necessary to outlaw an expanding force that refused army service but sought the second coming of its Messiah and the destruction of all except the faithful including, of course, the Roman empire.

The persistence of great numbers in the faith, however, promoted the revocation of the edicts of suppression within a decade. Most remarkably, after overcoming the last of his rivals in 323, Constantine acknowledged that his victory had been achieved under the sign of the True Cross of Christ (see volume

4, IMPERIAL SPACE, pages 114–115). Thereafter, the state fostered a catholic church as a new basis for imperial unity. It promoted the definition of canonical dogma, the development of a church administration in parallel to that of Diocletian's empire and the adaptation of the Roman basilica to Christian purposes with great magnificence (see volume 4, IMPERIAL SPACE, page 164).

Christianity apart, imperial unity was based on a common language, coinage and law, long-established patterns of trade and an international army. Primarily non-Roman, however, the army was inherently unreliable and economic development had produced self-sufficiency in the east by the 4th century. In the less-developed west, on the other hand, long the prey to unsettled barbarian forces, the old aristocracy entrenched itself at the expense of the impoverished, and it consolidated its estates as power bases independent of – even hostile to – the crumbling imperial regime.

Rome was sacked in 410 by the Visigoths and in 455 by the Vandals. The latter had taken North Africa; the former moved on through Gaul, taking Provence and Aquitaine, to occupy Iberia. Meanwhile, Burgundian tribes had settled in the Rhône Valley, northern Gaul was falling to the Franks, southern Germany to the Thuringians and Bavarians, the Saxons were spreading from eastern Germany to Britain and Slavic tribes were harrying the east. In 476, the last emperor of the west, Romulus Augustulus (475–76), abdicated under pressure from the Ostrogoths, whose king, Theodoric (493–526), ruled most of northern Italy from Ravenna. Fragmenting the Roman polity, tribes became nations – violently.

Secular building in a dark age

The four-square Roman camp, expansive of aspect (see volume 3, IMPERIAL FORM, page 125), vanished with the legions that had kept much of Europe under control for so long – if it had not, in fact, become a depressed town – and in the 'Dark Ages' that followed the fall of the empire in the west those with means retreated to towers on inaccessible crags. The contrast of mentality behind these two types of military architecture is stark. The former is positive and aggressive, easy to enter and leave on its open site, and asserts confident authority. The latter is negative and defensive, and provides for retreat through a succession of enclosures, behind rings of walls and beyond a range of obstacles along a tortuous line of approach, but it is vulnerable in its isolation and ultimately is at the mercy of outside forces – whether hostile ones forcing submission or friendly ones bringing relief.

In all civilisations from the earliest times this recourse has been obvious to man concerned with defence (see, for example, volume 1, ORIGINS, pages 88 and 214–215). Ultimately overcome by the enemy, or time, his lair rarely survives in its primitive state – especially in Europe. The line descends from the great citadels of the Mycenaean age (see volume 1, ORIGINS, pages 194–195 and 203) to the Greek Castle of Euryalus built to protect Syracuse on the east coast of Sicily,[2–4] to Byzantine Saône in Syria[5–6] and its European peers such as rebuilt Chinon in western France.[7] As secure bases for defending territory, rather than

2 **Syracuse, Castle of Euryalus** 4th century BC, from the east.

The key to the city defence works was begun by the tyrant Dionysius I (the 'Elder', 405–367 BC), at the western (inland) entrance to the site. It was strengthened by the usurper Agathocles (317–289 BC) and perfected by the mathematician and engineer Archimedes (c. 287–212 BC)

for the protection of the regime of Hieron II (c. 270–215 BC) against the onslaughts of Carthaginians and Romans. A succession of wards or compounds, circuitously approached, as here, was characteristic of the Mycenaean citadels. So too was a tower or keep providing limited but formidable accommodation towards the centre, though its full potential was far from being realised here as excavation in the rock below provided even less vulnerable living space.

3 Syracuse, Castle of Euryalus trench between the outer and middle zones, looking west.

The outer and middle zones were not merely walled but separated by a trench cut from the living rock. This was a device common to many later castles.

4 **Syracuse, Castle of Euryalus** detail of the northern
gate.

Deflection of the passage through several right-angles in
the restricted confines of a gatehouse was a ubiquitous
defensive device, forcing any adversary to expose a flank
while shifting his protective shield to right and left under the
watch of the defenders.

5 **Saône**.

The walls around the extensive plateau are Byzantine in origin and it is probable that Byzantine engineers excavated the great trench that cuts the plateau off from the neighbouring high ground. The castle was taken by Latin crusaders in the early 11th century; they added the square keep that controls the approach over the drawbridge probably in the early 12th century.

6 **Saône** ravine before main ward.

When the great trench was excavated, a slender pinnacle was left *in situ* to support the extended drawbridge.

7 OVERLEAF **Chinon** from the west.

The middle ward replaces a Roman fort. Some 10th-century masonry survives both there and in the western sector, the Château du Coudray, but most of the walls were rebuilt in the second half of the 12th century and augmented over at least two centuries.

8 **Marksburg**, burgfried.

The tower was rebuilt in the 13th century; the wings around the court retain 12th-century work. The complex was renovated in the 19th century.

retreats of last resort, these were certainly not without arrogance. More typical of the Dark Age norm, descended from the ubiquitous watchtower, is the Germanic burgfried that crowns so many crags along the Rhine – often also much rebuilt.[8]

In *De civitate dei* (*The City of God*, 413–26),[9] St Augustine (354–430) had predicted that the order of Christ's church was bound to prevail over even the most eminent of earthly ones, and in fact Rome fell within 40 years of the saint's death. In the dire circumstances of fragmentation that followed, the church found itself the sole instrument of supranational unity. Despite the significance of the imperial capital and the prestige of St Peter, primacy does not seem to have been accorded to the Bishop of Rome – the Pope – in the first Christian centuries, but recognition of the need for strong central government in the church preceded the abdication in 476 of Romulus Augustulus. Leo 1 (440–61) asserted primacy but it was not until Gregory 1, the Great (590–604), that Rome formally assumed the care of all the churches.

The hierarchy of bishops in authority over the dioceses and provinces of the Catholic church – and much of the property with which it had been endowed since Constantine promoted imperial faith in Christ – had emerged virtually intact from the collapse of the west-

9 **St Augustine,** *De civitate dei* (MS Canterbury, c. 1100, frontispiece; Florence, Biblioteca Laurenziana).

Converting Platonic metaphysics – and the Pythagorean mysticism which lay at its heart (see volume 2, HELLENIC CLASSICISM, pages 180–187) – to Christianity, St Augustine saw the City of God in terms of perfect number deduced from music. In his treatise on music, he defined the science of modulation in the arithmetical terms of ratio: the relationship between units of common measure or module. In accordance with Pythagoras, especially the determination of the divine significance of the four numbers of the first *tetractys* (1–4), he defines the intervals of the most perfect consonances as 1:1, 1:2, 2:3, 3:4 (symmetry, octave, fifth and fourth). As the intervals of the monochord are marked off by divisions on a string, their ratios may be represented as linear proportions which, in turn, may readily be seen as applicable to the visual arts. Indeed, subscribing to the Pythagorean concept of cosmic order as based on these ratios – of beauty as God-given number – St Augustine was bound to hear the eternal harmony of the divine in perfectly modulated music and to see it mirrored in architecture based on the same modulations: as music led reason towards the comprehension of God, so the church built in consonance with musical number must approximate God's City.

ern empire. The Roman concept of the county as the basic unit of provincial administration, paralleled by the church, also survived, though the town at its centre withered in the north, where counties became rural districts grouped with others under a 'duke' whose role combined those of Diocletian's diocesan vicar and the regional military commander (*dux*). Even the secular aristocracy, whose wealth and significance expanded in the last centuries of the empire at the expense of small-holders taxed out of existence, did not disappear in the chaos of the mid-5th century: involved in county and diocesan administration for generations, many of the old imperial magnates were retained by the new rulers in these capacities.

The rulers, on the other hand, had emerged from among the tribal warrior leaders who led the peripatetic Germans to new settlement, and needed land to sustain their pretensions. Sometimes this land was expropriated from the old Roman senatorial class, occasionally from the church, but many estates abandoned in the centuries of retrenchment were revived for the Germans. Sharing office in the service of state and church, entering the church to perpetuate its hierarchy, or marrying and merging their estates and riding together as the mounted élite at the head of the troops in war, the aristocracies of invader and invaded were united in little more than a generation. The fiscal privileges with which the magnates, lay and secular, were rewarded for service or support furthered the amassing of land at the expense of the lower orders, and their power waxed as the kings sapped their strength squabbling over incessant division of the kingdom in accordance with tribal custom.

Monasticism and conversion

The expansion of the church through the newly barbarised world depended on the monastery. Imported into Europe from Egypt in the mid-4th century (see volume 4, IMPERIAL SPACE, pages 130–131), monasticism was taken deep into Gaul soon after by St Martin, Bishop of Tours, who established a community near Poitiers. Another, established near Cannes in the early 5th century by St Honoratus, future Archbishop of Arles, was a major centre of Catholic ecclesiastical education. Many monks who graduated from there took the monastic ideal with them beyond Gaul, even as far as Ireland where St Patrick is believed to have introduced the faith in the mid-5th century.

Despite the shared instruction of many of their founders, the monastic communities of western Europe were largely unregulated until the 6th century, when St Benedict of Nursia (c. 480–547) – who was educated from, but retreated from, the decadence of post-imperial Rome – established his Order at Monte Cassino in southern Italy (see volume 4, IMPERIAL SPACE, page 132). Founded on earlier rules, but rejecting the extreme austerity of the earliest eastern communities, it is notable for its moderation and compassion in admitting basic human needs and acknowledging human weakness. It requires poverty, chastity, humility and communal harmony in complete commitment to the daily routine of four hours of study, five of labour, six of prayer, eight of sleep, and absolute obedience to the authority of the abbot.

Discipline and benevolent authoritarianism recommended St Benedict's rule to monasteries throughout Europe, dedicated to winning Rome's vanquishers to the new order of Christ. It was to the barbarian tribal leaders that Catholic monks went out to address themselves, of course, knowing that by winning the chief they would win the people – not only from paganism but also from heresy. Though there was some antipathy between the monks and the secular clergy of old-established parishes, the task was easier in deeply Romanised areas where Christianity was entrenched and the new rulers saw it as part of a superior culture.

The most significant gain was the conversion between 496 and 506 of the Frankish chief Clovis 1 (481–511) to the orthodox Catholicism of Rome rather than to the heretical Arianism favoured by other barbarian rulers. A century elapsed before Gregory the Great sent Augustine to convert the Anglo-Saxons, who seem to have eradicated whatever gains the Christians had made against the strong tradition of Celtic paganism under remote Roman rule. In the meantime, the vigorous Irish monks of the circle of St Columba (c. 521–97) had gone forth in 563 to convert the Picts in Scotland and to take the faith into England from the north. Many were to go much further and lead successful missions to Central Europe – such as St Columbanus (550–615) and his followers, one of whom founded the great abbey of St Gall in Switzerland.

The Merovingian Franks

Tribes of Salian Franks settled on the lower Rhine in the early 4th century and founded several principalities. Initially allied to Rome, Childeric I, son of Merovich, had led the principality of Tournai to predominance before his death c. 480. His son, Clovis I, overawed his rivals and established a kingdom based on Paris which confronted the Burgundians and the Visigoths of Aquitaine. The former eluded him, but the latter fell c. 507, and Visigothic Provence was taken by Theodoric. The new Salian state, called Merovingian after Clovis' grandfather, was recognised by the eastern emperor and its rise advanced the Catholic cause of the pope after the conversion of the king, though he asserted the right to appoint the bishops in his realm.

On his death in 511, Clovis' kingdom was divided in accordance with Frankish tradition between his four sons – roughly equitably but not viably. Allied with Theodoric they finally overcame Burgundy, and after Theodoric's death in 526 they took Provence, won Thuringia and established a dependent duchy of Bavaria in 555. As brothers died or were eliminated their lands were assimilated by the survivors. The extended kingdom was reunited under Clotaire I in 558 but divided again on his death three years later, and the resurgence of rivalry between the legatees fatally weakened them.

Gascons, pushed north from the Pyrenees by the Visigoths of Iberia, occupied the south-west. Lombards, who had taken north-western Italy from Theodoric's successors, raided the south-east. The Asiatic Avars, who crossed the Danube about the time of Clotaire's triumph, were attacking Thuringia before the century was out, and the Bavarians were asserting independence. By then the Merovingian domains were coalescing into two new states: Austrasia in western Germany and Neustria in northern Gaul. The two were reunited under Clotaire II in 613 but to secure support he ceded considerable power to the church and the secular magnates. After his son Dagobert I (629-39), the last effective Merovingian, a succession of weak rulers retained a fictional imperium but lost real power to the principal officers of state, the mayors of the palaces of Austrasia and Neustria. Meanwhile, Thuringia had been lost to the former, Aquitaine to the latter, and Provence was virtually independent in the early 8th century.

Church building in the Merovingian era

After the conversion of Clovis I, the Merovingians replaced temples with impressive churches on many of

France's enduringly important sacred sites. This happened in all the converted lands – in Britain actually on the order of Gregory the Great to Augustine (d. 604), who had implanted Christianity at Canterbury at the end of the 6th century. Despite the paucity of remains it is clear that antique buildings provided foundation and quarry for the Christian ones.

Typically early Christian church planning north of the Alps, as south, followed the basilican formula. All the most important churches have been rebuilt many times, of course. The oldest Christian building in France is the mid-4th-century baptistry of St-Jean, Poitiers but the contemporary foundations at St-Bertrand-de-Comminges (in the foothills of the Pyrenees) represent the implanting of a great tradition. The 5th-century substructure of St Martin, Tours reveals, further, that instead of the free-standing belfry common south of the Alps, towers were built over the crossing and on to the west end, not only to house the bells that advertised the times of mass, but also to provide the vertical aspiration that was so characteristic of northern architecture. The most substantial early survivor of the type with integral tower is the late 7th-century Anglo-Saxon church at Brixworth.[10–11]

10 **Brixworth, All Saints.**

Originally monastic, Brixworth was exceptionally large, its nave flanked with aisles or chapels. The foundations of spur walls between the nave arches makes the latter the more probable, i.e. that it was of the so-called compartment type. Beyond a square presbytery, the chancel seems to have been apsidal from the outset, later being surrounded by an ambulatory. The tower was originally of two storeys and probably gabled. The monastery was devastated by the Danes in the 9th century: when the church was restored for parish use in the 10th century the side spaces and ambulatory were abandoned but the western tower was raised and given a circular stair-turret. The apsidal chancel was replaced by a square one in the 15th century, but was restored in 1865.

In general, early northern churches were simple halls, not necessarily – indeed not usually – aisled like the prototypical basilica, and instead of an apse there would often only be a smaller hall projecting from the end opposite the door for the chancel. (The type, from which many English parish churches descend, is known, therefore, as nave-and-chancel.) There was often also a porch over which a tower might be built. The opening of lateral spaces for chapels occasionally produced the compartment church. Composition was a simple additive exercise.

Timber, not stone, was the natural medium of the forest-dwelling inhabitants of Britain. Masonry technology was introduced by the Christian missionaries in St Augustine's train for the rebuilding of a rare survival from the Roman period at the cathedral at Canterbury less than a century before the builders of Brixworth were deploying relatively

11 **Brixworth, All Saints** interior.

broad arches systematically. Those missionaries probably
produced an aisled basilica of the type familiar to them in
Rome for the first Canterbury, which is known to have had
a sanctuary raised over a crypt like S Pietro in Vaticano (Old
St Peter's), Rome. For the totally new church of St
Augustine's abbey, to the east of the cathedral, the aisles of
the standard basilica ceded to compartments. Not unique
(there were compartments at St-Bertrand-de-Comminges),
this was characteristic of the early English church, and
Brixworth may well have conformed.

The Carolingians

By the third decade of the 8th century the monastic orders had built the faith in western Europe into a bulwark against Muslim iconoclastic fervour from which a new force was able to turn the tide of invasion back against itself. Not 50 years earlier, in 687, the mayor of the palace of Austrasia, Pepin of Herstal (635–714), defeated his Neustrian peer and reunited northern Gaul – still nominally under the Merovingian king. In 714 Charles Martel, Pepin's illegitimate son, seized the initiative, soundly defeated the Neustrians again, asserted his authority over northern Gaul and restored Frankish dominion in the south. He then turned to confront the advancing Muslims, who had quickly overcome the Visigothic kingdom of Iberia after crossing from North Africa in 711, and repulsed them at Poitiers in 732. Charles went on to reclaim Aquitaine and to frustrate Muslim designs on Provence. He then reasserted Frankish authority over the Germans east to Thuringia and south in Bavaria. On his death in 741, the kingdom was divided between his sons, Carloman and Pepin the Short (751–68). In 747, after widespread rebellion, Carloman resigned his inheritance to Pepin who reasserted control, deposed the last of the

Merovingians and had himself elected king. Pepin then turned to Italy.

Italy, recovered from the barbarians by the great Byzantine emperor Justinian I (527–65) in the mid-6th century, was soon prey to a new tribe of barbarians known as Lombards. Byzantium controlled the sea and therefore the coastlands, but the Lombards had won most of the interior by the end of the 6th century and divided it into duchies for their commanders. They quickly began to assert their independence, but were brought to heel under a monarchy that accepted Christianity in c. 610. By the third decade of the 8th century the Lombard kingdom had absorbed most of northern and central Italy and its greatest king, Liudprand, was threatening Ravenna and Rome. Ravenna fell to Aistulf (749–56), and the Byzantine exarchate – the vice-royalty of the north – was extinguished in 751. Only the south remained to the empire but the Muslims were gaining ground there.

The pope, Stephen III (752–57) appealed for help from the Franks and they intervened decisively in 754, turning the fortunes of the Lombards and furthering the formation of a papal state in return for the pope's endorsement of Pepin's coup. In the process the nature of the Frankish monarchy was changed from a purely secular institution, originally elective but made hereditary by Merovingian pragmatism, to a quasi-sacred one held and inherited by divine right. In return for the pope's confirmation of legitimacy and bestowal of grace through coronation and anointment, the king was bound to rule with Christian virtue and the church could claim the superiority of the spiritual over the temporal power.

Pepin sealed the unity of most of the land that would be France with the expulsion of the Muslims from their remaining holdings on the Mediterranean coast. In Germany, on the other hand, the Bavarians were independent of him again by 763 and the Saxons remained unmollified. He died in 768 and was buried at St-Denis, north of Paris, where he had rebuilt the Merovingian abbey that became his tomb and was to become the necropolis of the French monarchy.[13] His kingdom was divided between his sons Charles and Carloman, but the latter renounced his rights and Charles (later Charlemagne) proceeded to take the Franks – and the Carolingian dynasty – to their apogee.[14] He retook Bavaria, defeated the Avars, succeeded in reducing the Saxons to vassalage, furthering

their conversion to Christianity, and established a firm eastern front against the Slavs. Though he secured the north against the obstreperous Danes, Charles was less successful in Spain.

After the fall of the Visigoths to the Muslims in Iberia, a small Christian kingdom had been founded in the Asturian mountains of Galicia. Alfonso the Catholic (739–57) began its southward expansion with faith in the aid of St James the Great who is believed to have brought Christianity to Galicia and whose tomb was identified in 813 at the place which thenceforth bore his name, Santiago de Compostela. Early in his career, Charles had failed both to inflict serious damage on the Muslims in Spain and to link up with the Asturians. After 801 he extended his authority to Catalonia but still failed significantly to diminish the Umayyad caliphate of Cordova.

Charlemagne (768–814) – as he was to be called[12] – believed he had been preferred by God to protect and prosper Christ's church. He supported papal attempts

12 **Charlemagne** bust in silver and gold made for the Holy Roman Emperor Charles IV (1347–78, crowned 1355) in 1350 (Aachen, Dom Museum).

to reform it, particularly to purge it of such venal practices as the sale of offices. He was ready support for Leo III (795–816) in Rome's running dispute with Byzantium over the perpetration of iconoclasm – indeed, it was this very issue that persuaded the pope to welcome a new empire in the west. Charlemagne stamped on all deemed heretical by Rome and promoted the regularisation of liturgy. He also fostered the revival of learning and the advancement of education through the church. On entering Italy to protect the pope from the Lombards, he took their capital at Pavia, assumed their crown and expanded the papal state at their expense. Leo III crowned him emperor on Christmas Day 800 and signalled the revival of the Roman Empire, on the basis not only of military might but also because of the new faith acknowledged by most Europeans. The church lent legitimacy to Charlemagne's rule and promoted its supranational triumph. Charlemagne lent efficacy to the papacy and promoted a truly Catholic church – as Constantine had done.

Charlemagne was acknowledged by the eastern emperor, Michael I (811-13), in 812 as emperor of the Franks, rather than the Romans, but he clearly considered himself to have revived the empire. He maintained the Frankish kingdom as a distinct entity, continued to wear the crown of Lombardy but guaranteed the autonomy of the Papal State within an Italian kingdom conferred on his oldest son, Pepin. Meanwhile, he had fostered the rebirth of imperial grandeur in his seat at Aachen (in modern Germany), emulating Rome but modelled on the chief glories of Ravenna.

Carolingian building

Adapting the legacy of the antique to modern needs, as in later renaissances, the Carolingian will to preserve the symbolism but to transform the substance was strong. With the progressive modernisation of the great cult centres – and the complete disappearance of some – the basis for the reconstruction of the new imperial architecture is provided by the great Palatine Chapel at Aachen, the tiny episcopal chapel at Germigny-des-Prés and the foundations of such works as the abbey of St-Denis,[13] the cathedrals at Autun and Clermont-Ferrand, and the churches of St Martin at Tours, St-Germain at Auxerre and St-Riquier. Well represented in an 11th-century image of the latter,[14] its most significant innovations were the distinguishing features of the great Romanesque church: its

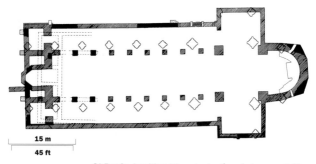

15 m
45 ft

13 **St-Denis, basilica** Merovingian foundations overlaid with Carolingian ones.

The church was founded c. 475 to enshrine the supposed remains of St Denis and was rebuilt from 754.

'westwork' for the reception of the emperor, incorporating the twin-towered gate or triumphal arch – the age-old symbol of ultimate power; its east end with multiple chapels for the celebration of numerous masses; its crucial transept separated from the sanctuary by a choir for the amplification of the chant – another great achievement of the age; its weighty walls and massive arcades surmounted by galleries in the westwork and probably over the aisles; and above all its imperial scale.

Built in 806, the little Greek-cross church of Germigny-des-Prés is still intact.[15–16] Attached to the palace of Theodulph, Bishop of Orléans, a member of the emperor's circle, it betrays the influence of the east and of the Muslim south – not surprisingly, perhaps, as the patron came from a part of south-western Gaul over which the Carolingians had long fought with the Muslims. In plan it is a quincunx, familiar in the Roman east at least since the 2nd century, but it predates the emergence of the form as standard for the churches of the Byzantine empire (see volume 4, IMPERIAL SPACE, page 224). As in the Moorish tradition imposed on Spain, but preceding most of the surviving buildings there, its arches – and most of its apses

14 **St-Riquier** engraved view of 1612 after the Hariulf MS drawing (1088) of the abbey church at about its consecration in 799.

A basilica c. 76 metres (250 feet) long, there were towers over the west entrance and the crossing, as in the original scheme for St Martin, Tours. In the 'westwork', vaults of outer and inner vestibules supported a high chapel dedicated to the Saviour: served by spiral stairs in twin turrets and surmounted by a triple-tiered spire, this aspiring space overlooked the nave through raised arcades. The account of the 11th-century chronicler Hariulf makes it clear that a boys' choir sang from galleries in the chapel in response to mens' choirs singing either side of a special space (known as the choir) at the crossing, before the apsidal sanctuary. Over the crossing a second great tower matched the western one. Beyond the cloister, to the south, a polygonal chapel dedicated to the Virgin and the Apostles seems to have been modelled on S Vitale, Ravenna (see volume 4, IMPERIAL SPACE, pages 202–204).

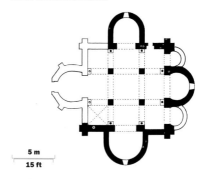

15 **Germigny-des-Prés** 806, extensively reconstructed 1867–76, plan.

The Greek cross in a square is defined by four central piers and an apse in the centre of each side – the western one pierced for the entrance. Framed with attached columns, the semidomical apses are linked by tunnel vaults to the central square, and small domes cover the corner spaces. The central superstructure has been rebuilt to a level lower than the original, but there seems always to have been a lantern tower typical of the north rather than a dome – which was typical of the eastern quincunx church.

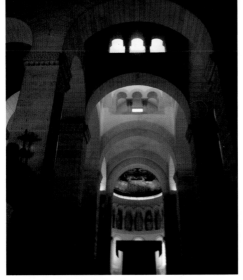

16 **Germigny-des-Prés** interior.
Above the arches supporting the central superstructure
are arcaded galleries that presumably reproduce in
miniature those through which the Saviour Chapel
overlooked the nave at St-Riquier (see 14, page 45).

in plan – are incurved like a horseshoe (see volume 6, FOUR CALIPHATES, pages 187–223). But its central tower is northern in derivation and, despite its size, its monumentality is imperial.

Outstanding by far, not only among the depleted remains from the time of Charlemagne but also from the early medieval period as a whole, is the octagonal Palatine Chapel of the palace complex at Aachen, now the cathedral.[17-19] Emulating what they took to be antique, Charlemagne's servants modelled it on S Vitale in formerly imperial Ravenna (see volume 4, IMPERIAL SPACE, pages 202–204). Emblazoned with the image of imperial power in the splendid mosaics of Justinian and Theodora, this vice-regal Byzantine work was understandably significant to a patron with imperial pretensions. No less significant, if somewhat more ironic, was the acknowledgement of the frontispiece of the so-called Palace of the Exarch, Ravenna (late 6th–7th century) as the archetype of the great palace, the symbol of a holy imperium (see volume 4, IMPERIAL SPACE, page 150).

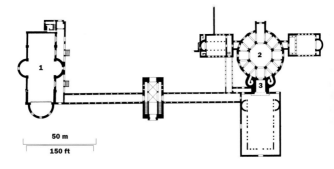

17 **Aachen, palace complex** 792–805, plan.

(1) Great Hall of State; (2) Palatine Chapel with Arch of
Appearance on the chapel façade (3).

Replaced by the town hall in the 14th century, the throne
hall (aula regia) was inspired by the late Roman basilica at
Trier (3rd–4th centuries) (see volume 4, IMPERIAL SPACE,
page 86), but given extra apses on the short north–south
axis.

18 and 19 (OVERLEAF) **Aachen, Palatine Chapel** exterior and interior.

The architect surpassed his model, S Vitale, in incorporating a westwork with an Arch of Appearance recalling that of the Exarch's Palace, Ravenna. From the central niche, the emperor could appear before his subjects assembled in the atrium below – as in the Arch of Appearance of the ancient twin-towered palace portal and the Roman triumphal arch. Flanked by cylindrical stair-turrets, the Arch of Appearance at Aachen opens off a throne room served by the first floor gallery, which enabled the imperial tribune to overlook the octagonal interior through arched colonnades. Over the throne room was a reliquary chapel, opposite it was a sanctuary for the emperor's worship above another opposite the entrance at ground floor level – these disappeared with the addition of the choir in the 13th century. Separated by wedge-shaped spaces, the eight compartments of the ambulatory are groin vaulted at base level and tunnel vaulted at tribune level. Tower-like, the central space has an octagonal canopy vault. Rich marble revetment and mosaic ensured that the building made no less an impression than the masterpieces of Justinian (see volume 4, IMPERIAL SPACE, pages 208–215).

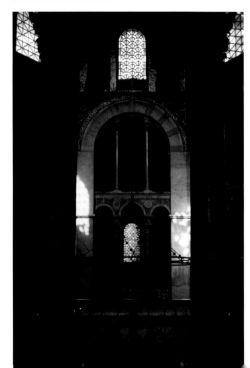

Charlemagne's empire did not long survive him, but it was to be emulated for a millennium. The greatest of the Franks had planned a tripartite division of his domains between his sons, but on his death in 814 only the youngest, Louis of Aquitaine (814–40), survived him. Surnamed 'the Pious' and surrounded by clerics on whom the significance of the pope's presence at his father's coronation was not lost, Louis saw his office as a sacred charge for advancing the catholic cause in a Christian commonwealth and had his coronation transformed into a sacerdotal ceremony centred on anointment. He systematised the administration, to the advantage of prelates who were appointed to oversee the civil administrators, and regulated the succession in favour solely of his oldest son, Lothair I (823–55), to preserve the unity of western Christendom. After his death in 840, however, his younger sons, Louis and Charles, challenged Lothair. By the Treaty of Verdun (843) the empire was divided: the western section (much of modern France west of the Rhône and Meuse) went to Charles, 'the Bald' (d. 877); the eastern section (much of modern Germany between the Rhine and the Elbe, plus most of Austria, Slovenia and Croatia) went to Louis, 'the German'

(d. 876); Lothair retained the imperial title and the middle section ('Lotharingia', stretching from Rome through Lombardy, Provence, Burgundy and Lorraine to The Netherlands).

In their contentions with one another and external invaders, Charlemagne's fractious successors bought support with counties, and great principalities were formed by the magnates of the west, as in the east. By 877, when Charles the Bald died, the main principalities were Aat least as significant as the royal domain around Paris. These were Flanders, assigned by Charles to his brother-in-law, Baldwin Iron Arm, in 862; Burgundy, detached from Lotharingia for Charles in the division of 869 and virtually autonomous after the further divisions of the kingdom after his death; Brittany, a Celtic preserve never wholly part of the Carolingian empire, unified under its first duke in the mid-9th century; Blois and Anjou, awarded to the magnate Robert the Strong by Charles in 861 to secure support in the struggle with the Viking Norsemen; Aquitaine, disputed by the heirs of Louis the Pious and autonomous after 877; and Toulouse, carved from the south by the counts Fredelon and Raymond from c. 850. Provence, part of Lothair's middle kingdom after 840, passed to his son, Louis, and asserted its independence on his death in 875.

Beyond the turmoil caused by rival claimants to shifting realms, there was the terror wrought by new waves of barbarian invaders, the Slavs and Magyars in the east and the Norsemen. The latter wreaked particular havoc on the church, not only striking on exposed coasts but also penetrating most of the major rivers of the north-west and east. They penetrated the lands that would be Russia from the Baltic to the Black Sea. They wintered periodically at the mouth of the Seine, formed a base there from which they threatened Paris in 845 and extended their rule over what was to be Normandy in 50 years. In the second half of the 9th century, too, they asserted Danish rule over the rival kingdoms that had been established by the Anglo-Saxons in eastern England. Their penetration of the Rhineland was the empire's undoing.

Magnates predominant

Lothair's dominions, divided between his three sons on his death in 855, had been redistributed among the remaining two by 875. After the passing of many contenders over the next decade, the empire was again united when Louis the German's son, Charles the Fat, took the west from Charles the Bald's infant grandson, Charles the Simple. Preoccupied – unfruitfully – with the incursion of the Norsemen into northern France, Charles the Fat failed adequately to defend the Rhineland and was deposed in 887 by Arnulf, the illegitimate son of his older brother, Carloman.

Arnulf too proved inadequate in defending the realm on two fronts: from Vikings in the north and from Magyar tribes pressing from the east. In 899, the tottering realm passed to his son, Louis the Child, and with him the eastern Carolingian line died in 911. Following Arnulf's example, the magnates holding the office of duke had already seized the initiative. The rump of Lotharingia acknowledged the Frankish king Charles the Simple, Franconia was the Carolingian heartland, while Swabia (settled by the Alemmani tribe) was disputed, but the Bavarian Liutpolds and Saxon Liudolfings, most exposed and successful against Danes and Magyars, eclipsed the undependable king in the confidence of their peoples.

On the death of Charles the Fat in 888, the year after he was deposed in the eastern realm, a conclave of western magnates elected to replace him with

Eudes, son of Robert the Strong of Blois and Anjou. In 893, rival magnates restored the Carolingian pretender, Charles the Simple, but he was certainly no more successful than his contemporary Arnulf in the east. The duchy of Normandy was ceded to the Norsemen in the fateful year 911 and, unable to control the magnates, Charles was deposed again in 922. He was replaced by Robert, brother of Eudes. The Carolingians reasserted themselves on Robert's early death, but his heir, Hugh, gained the title Duke of the Franks, and the Robertian line finally triumphed with the election of Hugh's son, Hugh Capet, in 987.

Spain

Meanwhile, from his capital at Oviedo, Alfonso III of Asturias (d. 914) had taken advantage of Cordovan disarray to extend his kingdom and to defend his eastern frontier with a chain of castles (after which a county established in the area was to be called Castile). His successor moved the capital south to León in 914, but a revival of Cordovan fortunes and the emergence of a Basque kingdom in Navarra under Sancho I (905–26) were sorely to challenge the Asturian ambition of restoring the Visigothic Christian kingdom in

Iberia. All three Christian states in the north – Asturias, or León as it was now called, Navarra and Catalonia, which had detached itself from the Carolingian empire as an independent county – had been subjected to the brutal rule of the Cordovan usurper al-Mansur by the end of the 10th century, but after his death in 1002 the threat of destruction receded. Instead, Sancho III of Navarra took the other Christian states: León and Barcelona became his vassals but Castile and Aragón were distributed to his sons as kingdoms on his death in 1035. León soon fell to Castile, and within 50 years Alfonso VI (1073–1109) had expanded his dominion south to Toledo, the ancient capital of the Visigothic kings – but provoked the intervention of the fanatical Moroccan Almoravids who re-secured the south and east.

Magnates and feudalism

Under undependable kings, dependence was on the one hand on personal bond – as it had been under undependable emperors in the late years of Rome – and on the other between tribal chiefs. The serf tied to the land – tilling it in summer, fighting on it in winter – was inherited from the destitution of the late empire.

The ever-present threat of reduction to serfdom thereafter drove vulnerable freemen to accept the bond of a lord for protection as his vassal. Others, dispossessed, contracted the land for use in return for service to a lord. Further up the social scale, the lesser aristocrat enrolled for service in the cavalry – which played an increasingly important part in the advance of the Carolingians – needed a patron to bear the considerable cost of horse and equipment. Sometimes it suited the lord to repay his vassal for past service with the grant of land as a benefice (fief) and in due course his tenancy became hereditary in return for hereditary service. The obligations incurred by the bond on both sides were acknowledged in the act of homage of client to patron, including an oath of fealty, and sealed in the investiture of client by patron with the fief. From the Latin *feudum* (for fief), this system of contractual relationships is known as 'feudal'.

Recalling the Constantinian caste system, perhaps, Charlemagne saw the advantage of cementing all the echelons of his imperial society in a pyramid of bonds – each man to a lord – with his own bond of protection at the apex. Under his undependable successors again, however, the pyramid disintegrated and bonds

subsisting on intrinsic logic became hereditary – like
tenancy and service. At the apex of his pyramid of
such bonds, the magnate aped the Merovingian king,
who had substituted the hereditary principle for election, and arrogated the administrative unit of duchy
or county to himself and his heirs as a sovereign preserve – at least in so far as the weakness of his nominal liege allowed.

This feudal system responded to and entailed
localised economy. Mediterranean trade had withered
if not with the disruption of the western empire by the
Germans in the 5th century, at least by the disruption
of the eastern one by the Muslims two centuries later.
Italy remained a bridgehead, partially Muslim in the
south, and trade continued to feed town life there
despite its diminution. The Frankish empire encour-
aged the development of trade in the north, and even
the disruptive Norsemen opened new routes. And
though many northern towns had withered in the age
of chaos, the agricultural economy of many counties
benefited from Carolingian unity, and flourishing
market centres provided the basis for the ultimate
revival of urban life.

Cluny

Monasticism was an essential element of this fragmented polity, indeed the survival of civilisation depended on the diligence of the studious monk.[1] By the end of Charlemagne's reign the main Benedictine stream was due for renaissance. At a synod held in 817 at Aachen under Louis the Pious, the Order was reorganised along lines determined at Aniane in Languedoc by the Abbot Benedict (c. 756–821) and the reformed rule was imposed on all the monasteries of his empire. Miraculously a contemporary document, probably a copy of the blueprint for a reformed monastic complex drawn up for Benedict and presented to the synod at Aachen, has survived in the monastic library at St Gall in Switzerland: it was adapted to that site as to many others in the empire.[20]

When the empire fell to the magnates, the Benedictines developed their own on the basis of the imperial systematisation of their rule. In 910, the year before the cession of Normandy and the disappearance of the eastern Carolingians, the Duke of Aquitaine endowed Abbot Berno of Baume-les-Dames and Gigny and his re-reformed Benedictines with a hunting estate at Cluny, in the Burgundian cen-

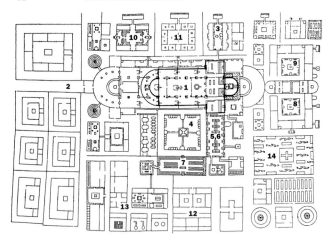

20 Ideal monastic plan c. 820 (Monastery of St Gall).
(1) Church; (2) entrance to monastic forecourt;
(3) abbot's palace; (4) cloister; (5–6) chapter house (below),
dormitories (above); (7) refectory; (8) novices' cloister;
(9) infirmary; (10) guest house; (11) school; (12) workshops; (13) service buildings; (14) burial ground as orchard.

Modular, the rectangular plan (460 by 640 Carolingian feet – of 30.4 centimetres per Carolingian foot) was conceived to be adaptable to level sites but was not in fact strictly followed in the construction of the monastery at St Gall. The double-apsed basilican church (c. 91 metres/300 feet long), comprehensively subdivided for multiple altars and maximum privacy for the monks celebrating mass, is towards the northern boundary and parallel to it, dominating the protected cloister (c. 30 square metres/100 square feet) to which its southern entrance is directly related. The main entrance to the site is from the west by a hostel for itinerants and a tethering ground for animals that also provide a barrier between the world at large and the enclosed world of the monk, centred on the cloister (as the name indicates). Further, the thin strip north of the church has other buildings related to the community served by the abbey, a guest house and school in particular; to the south is a cordon of workshops and service buildings. Framing the cloister are the main monastic living spaces, the dormitory and refectory, and beyond it to the east, furthest from the entrance, the rest of the monks' facilities – especially the infirmary and burial ground, which doubles as an orchard and vegetable garden in the economy of recycling.

tre of Lotharingia. Dedicated to the revival of St Benedict of Nursia's original spiritual ideal, lapsed again in
the century since Benedict of Aniane, they converted
the duke's villa into a new religious house that was
soon replaced on a grand scale. There they promoted
corporate worship in the splendour of sung mass as
much to celebrate God with all the resources
bestowed on man as to impress man with the fruits of
temporal power. And contrary to St Benedict's origi-

21 Cluny, second abbey church, known as Cluny II

c. 1050, plan.

   (1) Church; (2) entrance to monastic forecourt;
(3) chapter house; (4) abbot's palace; (5) cloister;
(6) dormitories; (7) refectory; (8) novices' cloister;
(9) infirmary; (10) guest house; (11) workshops;
(12) service buildings; (13) burial ground; (14) lady chapel.

   First installed in a villa, augmented with a church by 927,
the monks of Cluny began systematic rebuilding in 955. The
new basilican church, tunnel vaulted to provide the
optimum acoustic for choral chant, was dedicated in 981.
The complex is roughly square (c. 90 metres/300 feet per
side), but comparison with the St Gall plan (see 20, page 62) is
striking: the main difference is the designation of the chapter

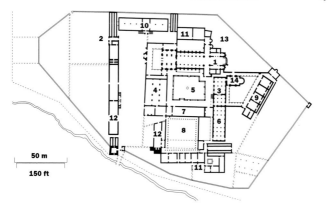

house (where those responsible for running the community deliberated) before a chapel dedicated to Our Lady to the east of the central cloister, the provision of a second cloister for novices to the south of the refectory (rather than by the infirmary) and the extension of the dormitory range along the east side of both cloisters. The completion of the scheme to accommodate 100 monks took a century.

nal rule, which envisaged the independence of each monastery, that power sprang from Abbot Berno's accumulation of abbeys and the extension of his authority as Abbot of Cluny over them and then over other abbeys to which Cluniacs took reform. Monarchical in structure, in accordance with the authoritarianism of St Benedict's concept of an abbacy, and bypassing episcopal and royal authority in its direct dependence on St Peter's Rome, Cluny was to extend a network of affiliated priories across Europe which promoted their abbot to power hardly inferior to that of an emperor.[21]

Though decadent in several respects, the Benedictine order generated the prime spiritual force in Christendom. Poor, chaste and obedient – in principle, if not always in practice – its monks and nuns were dedicated to the spiritual and physical health of all God's servants all over Europe. They housed the homeless, tended the sick and revived learning in many fields – medicine as much as theology, for instance – and imparted education to the poor as well as counsel to the rulers. They informed the beliefs of a society that, no matter how brutal, feared God.

Romanesque God and pilgrimage

God to the Romanesque Christian was the omnipotent, magnificent Pantokrator ('All sovereign'), vengeful judge rather than sacrificed saviour. And, furthering the early Christian anti-humanist mode of iconic art (see volume 4, IMPERIAL SPACE, pages 153–94), the Romanesque sculptor presented Him presiding in truly terrible majesty over the portals of Cluny's world.[22] Beneficent to the worthy, however, Christ was believed responsive to the intercession of His mother and the host of saints who had served and suffered for His Church. Consequently, the relics of saints (let alone of Christ's Passion) were highly prized. And pilgrimage to their shrines, particularly to the burial places of Old St Peter's, Rome and St James the Great, Compostela[23] (if not to the virtually unattainable Jerusalem), was the chief motive for medieval travel – other than war.

22 OVERLEAF **Autun, cathedral of St-Lazare** c. 1135, west portal

Christ in Judgement over the elect (to the left) and the damned (to the right) is flanked by St Michael in conflict with the Devil (right) and the apostles including St Peter with the keys to heaven (left).

Building under the later Carolingians

The prosperity brought by the relative security of empire and the ecclesiastical bent of the regime produced many churches. Spanning the territories ruled by Louis the Pious and his immediate successors, there are substantial representative remains at the three basilican churches on the island of Reichenau in Lake Constance, at Corvey on the Weser,[24] and in the crypts of St-Philibert-de-Grandlieu and the cathedral at Auxerre. Corvey is notable for its westwork,[25] the most complete example of the type from the Carolingian period, and also for the introduction of an ambulatory to the east end.[26] Early developments in catering for the passage of pilgrims through various curved and rectangular corridors is also revealed in the crypts of St-Philibert-de-Grandlieu,[27] St-Germain at Auxerre and the cathedral at Chartres. The definitive solution to the problem, with apse and concentric ambulatory serving radial chapels, was achieved in the rebuilding of the abbey of St Martin, Tours early in the next century.[28]

23 **Santiago de Compostela** sarcophagus in the crypt reputedly containing the remains of St James the Great.

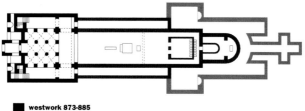

■ **westwork 873-885**

■ **consecrated 844**

■ **consecrated 867**

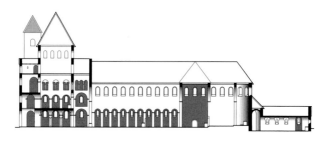

24 **Corvey, abbey** 873–85, plan and section.

Corvey was founded by monks from Corbie in Picardy in 822 as a centre for the further expansion of the faith to the east. They took with them the influence of St-Riquier (see 14, page 45), which then must have been the dominant complex in the region of their parent house.

Before its reconstruction in the late 17th century, the nave arcade was carried on simple rectangular piers, regularly repeated. Novel in Germanic lands for its date – but anticipated at Brixworth (see 10, page 32) – is the apse surrounded by an ambulatory, though the aisles continue past it to terminate in rectangular chapels, and a larger cruciform chapel is added to the centre.

25–26 OVERLEAF **Corvey, abbey** 873, westwork and interior of upper chapel.

The westwork is the most complete example of the type from the later Carolingian period, though the central part of the façade, between the side towers, was raised later to obscure its original central tower.

Above the vaulted vestibule, as at St-Riquier (see 14, page 45), the elevated chapel overlooks the basilica through an arcaded gallery.

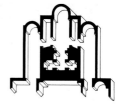

27 St-Philibert-de-Grandlieu c. 814–47, plans of crypt: c. 839 (left) and c. 847 (right).

At first, the sarcophagus of St Philibert was installed in an apse at ground level, below a raised sanctuary, entered along narrow corridors extending from the aisles to either side of the square presbytery. Then, as local pilgrimage to the relics of the saint developed rapidly, the narrow corridors were replaced with wider extensions of the aisles, terminating in apsidal chapels, and three more chapels were built beyond the apse en échelon (i.e. parallel to one another so that their walls resemble the rungs of a ladder in plan). The tomb chamber, originally subdivided awkwardly by the piers supporting the floor of the sanctuary and entered from the west through restricted openings to either side of a screen, was filled in to form a τ-shaped shrine entered from the east on axis with the central apsidal chapel.

28 **Tours, St Martin** dedicated 918, excavations of chevet.

The relics in the abbey church, taken to Auxerre in 872 to escape the Norsemen, were returned to a new church built after the removal of the Norse threat by the cession of Normandy in 911. The provision of corridors for pilgrims around three sides of a square shrine area at Auxerre, known to St Martin's entourage and presumably found less than felicitous by them, was replaced by a curve simply repeating that of the pierced apse, as at Chartres. There the relics were enshrined in the sanctuary at ground level, and the curved ambulatory around the apse at Chartres was screened from the sanctuary only by arcades so the pilgrims filing through the one could see the relics in the other

Beyond the empire, the Anglo-Saxons and the Celts of Britain and Ireland continued in their idiosyncratic way, largely building churches of the nave-and-chancel type, with or without compartments to each side and with or without attached towers. St Lawrence, Bradford-on-Avon is an early example.[29] There were, of course, great basilican cathedrals and abbeys, like those of Canterbury which had an apse at each end after the blueprint prepared for Benedict of Aniane (see 20, page 62), but these have disappeared under later rebuilding.

without entering it. There were apsidal chapels at the corners of the corridors at Auxerre. The radial arrangement around the circumference at Tours follows simple geometrical logic but its exact date is obscure.

By the end of the century the most extraordinary elaboration of the ambulatory, at St-Bénigne, Dijon (destroyed in the late 18th century), involved columns concentric with a huge rotunda clearly inspired by the Church of the Holy Sepulchre, Jerusalem (see volume 4, IMPERIAL SPACE, page 172). The church was a double-aisled, tunnel-vaulted basilica with a three-storey nave elevation including galleries as generous as the aisle arcades.

29 **Bradford-on-Avon, St Lawrence** 8th century, possibly rebuilt in the late 10th century.

Recorded in the 12th century as having been built by St Aldhelm in the early 8th century (but restored c. 975 to a degree over which there is some controversy), the chapel originally consisted of a small, tall nave (c. 7.6 by 4 metres/ 25 by 13 feet but c. 7.6 metres/25 feet high) with projecting porches and an even smaller chancel, separated by narrow doors and lit by slit windows placed high in the walls.

Apart from the nave-and-chancel type, the Anglo-Saxons occasionally built churches in which the tower was the main element. This seems to have been the case at Earls Barton.[30] Viking invasions destroyed the cultural life promoted by the monasteries, and little English building remains for the two centuries between Brixworth and Earls Barton. During that time, however, the insular Saxons developed idiosyncrasies that were to mark English architecture throughout its history. These appear in the churches built after Dunstan

30 **Earls Barton, All Saints** second half of the 10th century, tower from the south-west.

The present aisled church is much later than the tower: the quoins are complete on all four corners, suggesting that the original nave or chancel attached to the east side was narrower – as at Barton-on-Humber. As in the latter work, too, a network of string courses and slim pilaster strips, incorporating semicircular and triangular elements, manages to be both rich and naïve. In contrast with the blind arcading, the door and most of the windows are framed with weighty arches, several with stocky columns and intrados carved from lintel blocks rather than constructed with voussoirs.

of Glastonbury promoted monastic revival and reform in the mid-10th century, under the inspiration of contemporary developments on the continent. Little is left from the period, but it is assumed to have been conservative except for its wayward, anti-architectonic decoration. The web spun of attenuated structural forms and applied irregularly out of context to the Earls Barton tower is characteristic. And columns bulge with a soft plasticity: those of Earls Barton are typical, but at its most extreme in the crypt at Repton church, the bulge needs to be contained with spiral binding.

Unlike Saxon England, Christian Spain is comparatively rich in varied forms. S Julián de los Prados, in the Asturian capital Oviedo, may be taken as representative of the basilican norm – though it was exceptional in decoration.[31] Several works from late in the century display the horseshoe arch characteristic of the so-called Mozarabic style developed from their experience of Moorish architecture by Christian refugees

31 **Oviedo, S Julián de los Prados** c. 830, longitudinal section.

A basilica with a dominant transept, this was a palatine church linked with the residence of Alfonso the Chaste

(791–842): presumably part of his apartment, the king's tribune overlooked the north transept through a large window. The tunnel-vaulted sanctuary is flanked by parallel chapels (en échelon). The nave, screened from the transept with an arch matching the proscenium of the sanctuary, has three arched bays with simple rectangular piers surmounted by a clerestory. Nave and transept are painted with feigned aedicules in an unexpected re-evocation of the late Pompeian style (see volume 3, IMPERIAL FORM, pages 168–169). Except for the sanctuary, the roofs are wooden, but the near-contemporary hall church of S María, Naranco (consecrated 848) is entirely tunnel-vaulted over a blind arcade in which the graded arches are slightly incurved.

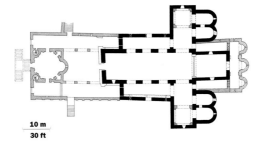

10 m
30 ft

32 **Cuxa, S Michel** c. 955, plan.

A rectangular sanctuary continued the lines of the nave arcade beyond an extended transept with twin apsidal chapels to each arm. After 1010, a rectangular ambulatory with three apsidal chapels encapsulated the sanctuary, twin towers were built over the end transept bays and a narthex preceded by a quatrefoil Trinity Chapel was added to the west. Somewhat modified in the 11th century, the original style was Mozarabic as at S María, Ripoll where an even grander vaulted basilica with apsidal sanctuary was begun c. 977. There was no ambulatory at Ripoll, but in the smaller contemporary church of S Pere de Roda near Gerona (consecrated 1022) the apse opened through arcades to a semicircular ambulatory.

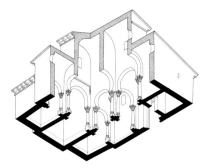

33 **Lebeña, S María** 924, cutaway and worm's-eye view axonometric.

A variation of the quincunx produces a square nave and sanctuary before and beyond an oblong crossing, smaller square transept arms, oblong chapels either side of the sanctuary, square ones either side of the nave and an oblong narthex flanked by square chapels. All the arches are incured except for the profiles of the tunnel vaults which run longitudinally over an interpolated clerestory for the nave, crossing and sanctuary, laterally for the lower subsidiary spaces. Columns are attached to the piers as they were to the walls of S María, Naranco and, indeed, to the piers of Germigny-des-Prés.

from the Caliphate of Cordova. The outstanding basilican examples, S Miguel de la Escalada near León, S Michel, Cuxa[32] or the abbey of S María, Ripoll in Catalonia, span much of the 10th century, but the form was widely approximated in churches and synagogues converted from mosques of the same style. From the early 10th century, too, there was considerable variation on the Greek cross plan of Germigny-des-Prés and the Byzantine east.[33]

The Italians sustained the early Christian tradition throughout the Carolingian period, as they were largely to do for a long time after. However, the Lombards were responsible for considerable developments, particularly in masonry techniques and the organisation of masons into a regulated guild. The process of regularisation seems to have begun in the mid-7th century and on its basis not only were the technical advances achieved but also *lambardos* became synonymous with the mason throughout Europe.

The Lombards are often credited with effecting the transition from the Carolingian 'renaissance' to a 'first Romanesque' – though the former might as well be seen as the latter. Apart from the improvement in masonry marked by the reintroduction of dressed stone in small blocks, rather than the rubble of a darker age (if not of Aachen), the major characteristics of their work were the tauter integration of still-autonomous parts, nave arcades carried on piers articulated with pilasters rather than on columns, and corbel tables fringing eaves. The basilica was most usual here as elsewhere and the influence of Old St Peter's, Rome was predominant.

Perhaps the major contribution of the Lombards to medieval architecture was the development of the groin vault instead of the wooden roof or masonry tunnel – especially over the chancel where it simulated the canopy of the imperial throne appropriated for the Vicars of Christ. While the tunnel vault admits light only from the ends and needs thick walls to support it, the groin vault is carried by four arches over a rectangular bay that may be lit from all sides and buttressed by the counter-opposition of forces in a series of such bays rather than by the dead weight of massive masonry. Unprecedentedly sophisticated in their command of the dynamics of structure, the Romans made the transition from the one to the other on a grand scale under the emperor Trajan (98–117) in the early 2nd century (see volume 4, IMPERIAL SPACE, page 61). After the Dark Ages that obliterated such sophistications, the Lombard heirs of the Romans made a similar transition for the apsidal chapels and chancels of basilicas.

From the limited survivors, S Pietro, Agliate (c. 875) and Sant'Abbondio, Como are generally singled out – though the latter was rebuilt in the 11th century. Nave and aisles at S Pietro terminate in apses, the two side ones preceded by groin-vaulted chapels, the central one by a tunnel-vaulted chancel. Beyond its wooden-roofed nave, flanked by double aisles like the basilica of Old St Peter's, Rome, Sant'Abbondio preserves Italy's oldest-known groin-vaulted chancel, buttressed by twin belfries.

The legacy of the Carolingians

The Carolingian age bequeathed a style of building that, given the overwhelming cultural legacy of ancient Rome – not least the supreme skill of its engineers in spanning space with the semicircular arch, and the vaulting derived from it – was inevitably Romanesque. It was created to proclaim a political ideal as much as to glorify God and accommodate the faithful. These were perfectly consistent to a ruler like Charlemagne, let alone Louis the Pious: indeed the achievement of the great church was due to the patronage of church and state. The cathedral depended on royal patronage, but dynasts endowed abbeys too, of course, though in general the role of the monastery as builder was paramount. Beyond court circles, funds were readily proffered by those seeking indulgence, and pilgrimage provided the channels for ideas as well as the occasions for the proliferation of church-building projects.

These projects were bound to be diverse. Ideology apart, feudalism naturally promoted the development of distinct schools of Romanesque architecture within the diversified realms of Europe. The differences between regions within Europe and, indeed, between two broad phases of development across Europe, may be seen in use of materials, in approaches to massing and in richness or austerity of form and decoration. But behind the diversity lay community of aim. Above all, the great church was an enduring structure: this meant, ideally, that it was of stone, and sophistication in the handling of stone – particularly the transition from rubble to small dressed blocks (petit appareil) to monumental ashlar (grand appareil) – was acquired through reference to Roman antiquity.

If the regular colonnade, clerestory and revealed

timber roof truss of the early Christian basilica was long to survive, particularly in Italy, northern builders were overwhelmingly impressed by the superimposed arcades of the ancient aqueducts or arenas as models for their main interior elevations. They enhanced monumentality and security by re-mastering all the Roman vaulting techniques – tunnel, groin, domical (see volume 3, IMPERIAL FORM, page 183) – and by replacing columns with piers they varied the rhythm of the main arcades. Antiquity also provided a repertory of decorative detail, and its literal translation in areas with prominent Roman remains was a principal characteristic of the high Romanesque. More usually, and more abundantly when the mastery of masonry took the style to its apogee, the abstract order of antique humanism is eclipsed by the didactic representationalism of Christianity.

Apart from building types, techniques and ornament, the Romans also provided the principal motifs of Christian architecture – above all the triumphal arch. Marking the apotheosis of emperor or hero, the form of the triumphal arch was abstracted from the twin-towered portal of the ancient Mesopotamian palace, the place of epiphany of the divine ruler (see volume 1, ORIGINS, page 84), through the intermediacy of the Hellenistic rulers who preceded the Romans. Of obvious symbolic relevance to a faith centred on the concept of resurrection, the triumphal arch as the church door presided over by Christ the Judge was the most powerful theme of Romanesque art.

Beyond the triumphal arch, palace imagery always pervaded the Christian concept of the church – as a building apart, the institution of God's elect, above all as the image of God's heavenly mansion to which it was the door. And the concept of Heaven as a palace prefigured here on earth by the church was sustained throughout the Middle Ages: with it went the idea of God as the supreme architect and the dedication of the church builder to emulate the perfection of His work as defined by St Augustine in *De civitate dei* (see 1, page 6).

On the death of Louis the Child in 911, the German dukes who had seized the initiative re-instituted the principle of election to the monarchy and chose Conrad of Franconia (911–18) – not without dissension. *Primus inter pares*, Conrad had to prove himself and failed. On his death in 918, power passed to the Saxons with the election of the Liudolfing Duke Henry the Fowler (919–36). Opposition from Swabia and Bavaria was overcome and Henry's military prowess confirmed him in authority over all Germany. His personality alone checked the autonomy of the secular magnates, but he promoted ecclesiastical ones to the principal officers of state. Before his death he had gained the initiative in the east by turning back the Hungarians. A decade earlier he had laid the foundations for Saxon ascendancy in the west with the re-acquisition of Lotharingia.

To protect the realm from barbarian incursion – and internal opposition – Henry revived Roman fortification where possible and constructed a series of fortress towns. These usually consisted of a citadel on high

34 **Otto II** c. 983, manuscript illumination by the master of the *Registrum Gregorii*, Trier (Musée Conde, Chantilly).

ground overlooking the surrounding terrain and protecting a ward for the rehoused local population – after the pattern long adopted on the much smaller scale of the individual land holder.

On the basis of his father's achievement, Henry's son Otto I, the Great (936–73) re-established the empire. He defeated the dukes of Franconia, Lotharingia and Bavaria who had united against him, keeping the Franconian counts under direct control, like the Saxons, and delegating the others to close relatives. As counties fell vacant elsewhere, he retained or bestowed them on the church to counter the power of the secular aristocracy. He crushed the Magyars in 955 but failed permanently to extend Saxon authority – and Christianity – to the Slavs. He gained Lombardy by marriage in 951 and returned to Italy in 962 to be crowned emperor by the teenaged pope, John XII (955–64). Otto confirmed imperial protection of the papal state and expanded it. However, the papacy had descended to venality under the influence of the Roman aristocracy, and the next year he deposed the disreputable pope John for treachery, asserted the right to ratify papal elections and chose the next two popes – Leo VIII (963–65) and Benedict V (964–66). He reached an accord with the eastern emperor Romanus II (959–63) whose daughter, Theophano, married his son in 972. That son acceded as Otto II (born 955) the following year.[34]

Otto II, Otto III (983–1002) and Henry II (1002–24) sustained the Saxon empire for half a century. They travelled incessantly to check the local magnates and to assert their authority wherever they stopped, and furthered the policy of transferring power from the hereditary secular aristocracy to ecclesiastical magnates whose celibacy was meant to prevent its permanent arrogation. In particular, counties were given to the church, thus undermining the power of the duchies. Meanwhile, the king, who appointed the bishops and prelates, continued to provide the principal officers of state. If only in virtue of this interdependence of church and state against the secular magnates, the Ottonian domain came to be called the 'Holy Roman Empire'. And the Saxon kings, especially the theocratic Otto III, acknowledged that interdependence at the highest level in partnership with the pontiff: they offered protection to and accepted the crown from the pope in Rome. Like Charlemagne, and like Louis the Pious, they were anointed.[35]

35 **Crown of the Holy Roman Empire** made for Otto I
but given the arched band and enlarged cross by Otto III
(Schatzkammer, Vienna).

On the death of Henry II, the crown passed to the
Rhenish Salian Franks with the election of Conrad II
of Speyer (1024–39). After overcoming various chal-
lenges he was crowned king of Italy in Milan in 1026
and emperor in Rome the following year. His major
territorial gain was Burgundy, left to him on the death
of its childless duke in 1032, but he won back lands
lost to the Poles. His son and successor, Henry III (d.
1056) concentrated on further increasing the independence of the crown at the expense of the nobility
and to the profit of a dependent church. This provoked
reaction from both sides: ecclesiastical reformers who
disclaimed lay authority over the church; and the
nobility, disenchanted not only with the rich endow-
ment of churchmen but also with the preferment to the
imperial entourage of a knightly class from below its
own ranks, which asserted itself as the emperor's powers began to fade with illness and his judgement in
bestowing fiefs faltered. At its height, however, those
powers were impressively displayed in the great palace
complex that the emperor developed as his principal
residence at Goslar.[36]

Henry III sought to extend his control over the
church, from the appointment of bishops to the elec-

36 **Goslar, Pfalz, the palace of Henry III** 1050, rebuilt in part 1132, restored 1873.

One of several similar palaces, but reputedly the peripatetic emperor's favourite base, the main building consists of a great hall over service rooms. It is attached to the south to the chapel of Our Lady built by Conrad II c. 1035. The throne was probably always placed in the great

tion of the popes: descending on Italy for his imperial coronation in 1046 he found it deplorably degraded once more. He dismissed the dissolute thrice-elected Benedict IX (1032–44, 1045, 1047–48) and two anti-popes in favour of his German nominee, demanded the decisive vote in future conclaves, ensured the accession of three more German popes and excited a reform movement within the church – inspired by the reformed Cluniacs – that was to react against him. The reforming emperor chose a reformer in Leo IX (1049–54) who immediately denounced the sale of ecclesiastical offices and condemned lay interference in the appointment of bishops. To eliminate abuse and regularise church practice in accordance with an established canon of ecclesiastical law, Leo asserted papal primacy unequivocally and led the church to its great

hall's wider central bay, but Henry III's building seems to have been unbroken by a central transept, at least at roof level: stressed in the 19th-century reconstruction, this may have originated in the rebuilding of 1132. Probably at that time, too, imperial apartments and the centralised chapel of St Ulrich were added to the north of the great hall and joined to it by a gallery.

schism primarily over the wording of the creed – the Byzantines maintaining that the Holy Ghost proceeds from the Father alone, while the Romans credited both the Father and the Son. And Leo's successors continued the reform process with even greater vigour, limiting papal election to the college of cardinals, though admitting confirmation to the emperor, and proscribing lay investiture of bishops. Then in 1075 Gregory VII (1073–85), believing that secular intrusion had corrupted clerical life and that healing would flow only from the spiritual authority of the pontiff, declared papal infallibility.

Though Henry III began the reform process, the edicts of Leo IX and his successors against secular involvement in church affairs denied the emperor his main weapon against the magnates. This was not effectively challenged during the minority of Henry IV (1056–1106), who succeeded his father when a small boy, but the new emperor attempted to regain the initiative by declaring the pope deposed early in 1076. The pope responded by excommunicating the emperor, absolving his subjects of their oaths to him. Dethronement threatened. Doing penance, barefoot in the snow, to the pope at Canossa in 1077, the emperor was readmitted to the church but, ceding to the pope's authority, he lost his cause and the confidence of the major German magnates – especially the Saxons – who proceeded with the dethronement. The Salian Rhineland remained loyal, so too did most of the bishops and several important southern vassals, and Henry forged an alliance with the common people. On this basis, and with a staunch chain of castles in the Herz mountains of central Saxony,[37-38] he survived to wage a 20-year struggle which exhausted the resources of both sides and divided the German church whose lands were widely pillaged for recompense. It ended only when Henry's son entered the fray against him in 1105 and succeeded him the following year as Henry v (1106–25).

The crown gained strength from its alliance with the people against the nobles, but it lost it in the alliance of the heir with the princes against his father and was never to recover the authority ceded to the pope at Canossa. Henry v resumed the struggle with the papacy and the princes, overawed the pope, Paschal II (1099–1119) and forced his own coronation, but was unable to regain permanent supremacy over papacy or princes, especially the Saxons. The princes emerged as

37 **Herzburg** c. 1073, model (waiting room of Herzburg cable car).

The irregular enclosure was dominated by a stout cylindrical watchtower, but the imperial accommodation was in a rectangular block behind. The power of the Ottonian and early Salian emperors had ensured that castle building was much rarer in Germany than elsewhere in feudal Europe, until the investiture crisis in the second half of the 11th century. The earlier watchtowers were usually square in plan, but cylindrical stair-turrets were common in ecclesiastical westworks.

38 **Herzburg** remains on site.

arbiters in the recurrent struggle over investiture and brokered a compromise that conceded the canonical election of bishops in return for the ruler's right to endow the elected bishop. On his death, Henry left a weakened monarchy to which his principal Saxon opponent, Lothair of Supplinburg (1125–37), was elected in his stead.

The imperial church

In line with the aims of the Saxon dynasty to restore coherence to their domains through military might and to sustain it in the catholicity of the church, the imperial will promoted a relatively homogeneous style of ecclesiastical architecture across the lands that now constitute Germany. Fundamental to this was a tauter integration of the parts of the church which had emerged as standard from the Carolingian achievement: the wooden-roofed basilica with many towers, westwork and extra sanctuaries for more masses, like at Corvey (see 24–26, pages 72–75). On an even grander scale, composition was still additive, but the semicircular geometry of the ambulatory, defined at Tours (see 28, page 77), disciplined the process and a framework of pilasters or attached columns, anticipated at Germigny-des-Prés (see 16, page 47), bound together the parts. Beyond western imperial inspiration, moreover, Byzantium contributed the richness of varied rhythm to internal elevations.

The Saxon emperors asserted authority with grand new cathedrals throughout their domain, but their particular concern was to build bastions of the faith as bridgeheads to the pagan east. The greatest example was Otto the Great's cathedral at Magdeburg, but – like the contemporary cathedrals at Mainz and Worms in the Rhenish west of his empire – that disappeared in subsequent rebuilding. The grandest surviving representative of the type is the convent church of St Cyriakus, Gernrode.[39-40] There the influence of works like S Demetrios, Salonica (originally late 5th century) is discernible in the alternating rhythm of columns and piers in the nave arcade and the introduction of triforium gallèries (see volume 4, IMPERIAL SPACE, page 181). Pilaster strips and decorative arcading under the eaves derive from Lombardy.

The later addition of a western apse at St Cyriakus conformed to the Aniane blueprint for church planning of 817 (see 20, page 62). The second apse could accommodate an additional choir and, hence, provide

39 **Gernrode, St Cyriakus** begun 961, from the west.

Over a reduced narthex, eliminated with the addition of the western apse, the westwork is less massive than at St-Riquier or Corvey (see 14 and 24–26, pages 44 and 72–75), dispensing with the central tower and upper chapel, and substituting cylindrical stair-turrets for the square side towers (as at St Pantaleon, Cologne where a portico has been added instead of an apse).

40 OVERLEAF **Gernrode, St Cyriakus** nave looking east.

Aisled basilicas with transepts were the Ottonian norm, but there were exceptions – like the contemporary St Pantaleon, Cologne (966–80). The triforium galleries at St Cyriakus are the earliest significant examples in Germany and the form was not subsequently popular there: Greek in origin, like the richly varied capitals of the nave arcade, it is possible that they were introduced here as secluded accommodation for the inmates of the convent at the instigation of the patron, Otto II's Byzantine wife, Theophano. The ambulatory, which made a putative appearance at Corvey (see 24, page 72) to discipline the additive composition of the east end, was not repeated here and it was largely undeveloped in Germany.

for polyphony: the form recurs often in imperial churches, most notably in the generation after the completion of St Cyriakus, at the cathedral at Mainz (see 49–50, pages 122, 123) and at St Michael, Hildesheim, where the twin crossing towers, flanked by twin turrets, and alternating rhythm of the nave arcade mark the achievement of a Romanesque ideal.[41–43]

The original plan of St Cyriakus, with a transept before the sanctuary raised over a crypt in the apse, recalls Old St Peter's, Rome at least after its high altar was raised c. 600. Imperial pretension recommended the Constantinian church as the pre-eminent model for the great metropolitan churches of the revived empire, but, of course, Charlemagne's Palatine Chapel, Aachen (see 18–19, pages 48, 49) – and through it Justinian's S Vitale, Ravenna (see volume 4, IMPERIAL SPACE, pages 202–204) – were also often emulated. Apart from St Cyriakus, the Ottonian cathedral at Mainz was a major example of the former. Also, the westwork at Essen, begun under Otto II c. 980, is based on half the Aachen octagon and achieves the full form as it rises in association with a square tower flanked by cylindrical stair-turrets. Quite different, and prophetic of the future rather than retrospective,

41 **Hildesheim, St Michael** begun 1001, dedicated 1015, completed 1033, from the south-east.

In the external massing, towers proliferated in accordance with the early Romanesque additive approach to composition, but their disposition dominated the parts. East and west ends are similar in their massing except for a slightly shorter bay before the eastern sanctuary and a passage around the western apse serving the crypt. There is no crypt to the east.

42 **Hildesheim, St Michael** interior, looking west.

As the two apses were original, the church was entered
through the south aisle as in the blueprint for the abbey
church devised for Benedict of Aniane where access was
directly from the cloister. There are no galleries except at the
ends of the transepts where they could accommodate choirs
for enhanced polyphony.

43 **Hildesheim, St Michael** interior, east end.

is the westwork of the Ottonian cathedral at Strassburg which, like the near-contemporary west end of Cluny II, dispenses with the typical Carolingian central tower-block flanked by a pair of stair-turrets in favour of twin towers.[44]

With the accession of Conrad II of Speyer and the Salian line the centre of architectural gravity was definitely the Rhineland. Indeed, it was at Speyer where the new emperor began work on a great new church as a dynastic shrine.[45-46] Here, the imperial model, in scale as in much else, was the great late Roman basilica at nearby Trier (see volume 4, IMPERIAL SPACE, page 86). Down the length of the nave arches are superimposed to monumental effect, as there and in a typical Roman aqueduct. Moreover, as on the exterior of the Trier basilica, a colossal arcade is stamped on each bay to full height, but here it is articulated with slender half-columns. The east end was conservative, without chapels en échelon or ambulatory, but it was raised over the most magnificent crypt of the period[47] and crowned with an octagonal tower at the crossing. There was no apsidal choir to the west but a westwork of the Carolingian kind – befitting the pretensions of a new imperial dynasty from Franconia.

44 **Strassburg, cathedral** begun c. 1015, west front,
reconstruction.

The westwork has ceased to be a self-contained block:
the triple arcade in the centre led through a porch directly to
the nave. The towers flanked the porch and the twin doors
at their base led through square chambers to the aisles.

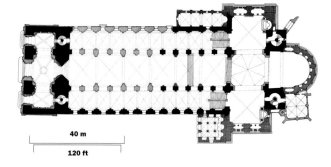

45 **Speyer, cathedral** c. 1030–65 and 1082–1106, plan.
Conrad II rebuilt the abbey church at Speyer on an
exceptionally grand scale – and with grand appareil – as a
necropolis for his dynasty. The sanctuary is raised over a
crypt after the precedent set at Old St Peter's, Rome.

46 **Speyer, cathedral** reconstruction.

The westwork retained the central tower but displaced the twin rectangular stair-turrets from the ends to the eastern side where they terminate the aisles. There is an apse only at the east end beyond the square crossing and square arms of the transept.

47 **Speyer, cathedral** crypt.

The crypt, built in the first campaign of work under Conrad II, extends under the transept as well as the sanctuary and, naturally, provides the basis for their division: each of the three compartments under the transepts is divided by four columns into nine groin-vaulted bays, and an extension of the system supports the sanctuary.

48 PREVIOUS PAGE **Speyer, cathedral** vaulted 1062, ruined in the 17th century, rebuilt subsequently, nave.

In the vast nave (c. 72 by 14 metres/235 by 45 feet and c. 27 metres/90 feet high), originally roofed in timber but flanked by groin-vaulted aisles, the Ottonian alternating rhythm of piers and columns is abandoned. The regular succession of massive piers is articulated with attenuated half-columns from which blind arches soar up over the aisle arcade to frame the clerestory, after the example of the exterior of the late Roman basilica at Trier (see volume 4, IMPERIAL SPACE, page 86). There is no triforium gallery.

Henry IV began the vaulting of the nave at the height of the investiture dispute with Gregory VII with obvious didactic intent. The insertion of groins hardly precedented in scale since antiquity – at least north of the Alps – required the strengthening of alternate piers: transverse arches, separating the paired bays, are supported by two tiers of superimposed columns, sturdier than the originals and attached to pilaster-like projections. The lateral arches enclose a second clerestory. Though there were antique groin vaults in the Rhineland that could have provided models for the Salian architects, Henry may have brought the idea back from Italy. Pilaster strips and a gallery under the eaves suggest a northern Lombard influence.

Henry IV transformed Speyer after 1082 by replacing the original timber roof with a series of groin vaults over paired bays, the definitive piers of which required considerable strengthening.[48] Inspiration may well have been found at first hand in such northern Lombard churches as S Pietro, Agliate or Sant' Abbondio, Como.

The other major Rhenish cathedrals of Mainz[49-50] and Worms have also had chequered histories, the latter marking the development of triapsidal sanctuaries perhaps inspired by the quatrefoil form of S Lorenzo, Milan (see volume 4, IMPERIAL SPACE, pages 184–185). Most of the great imperial churches have changed over time, but the purest image of Salian Romanesque is provided by the abbey of Maria Laach,[51-52] and, so far as its silhouette is concerned, by the cathedral at Tournai,[53] though that is outside the Salian field.

The scale and monumentality of Conrad's work, inspired by the remains of Roman imperial greatness, is matched by an austerity which certainly did not spring from paucity of resource. The impulsion, rather, was the force of a conviction rooted in the concept of the church as the scene of man's encounter with tran-

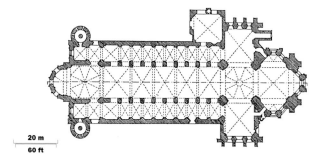

20 m
60 ft

49 **Mainz, cathedral** late 12th century, plan.

First rebuilt on a grand scale under Otto II from 978, burnt at its dedication in 1009, rebuilt and reconsecrated by 1036, rebuilt again 1060–1137 and yet again 1181–1239, the cathedral has been much developed since, but on the Ottonian basis. Like Old St Peter's, Rome, the high altar was at the western rather than the eastern end, but there was no crypt. Like that great model, too, there was one apse beyond one great transept, here endowed with an octagonal lantern tower at the crossing, which was later heightened. After the manner of St Cyriakus, Gernrode (see 39 and 40, pages 106–9) and St Pantaleon, Cologne, a second apse was added to the east front and stair-turrets to both ends in the rebuilding

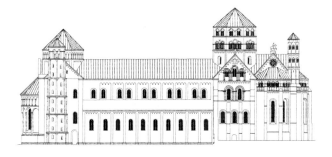

50 **Mainz, cathedral** from the north, reconstruction.

before 1036. The eastern transept may date from that time, in inception at least, but it was with the construction of apses at its ends, matching the sanctuary in a trefoil form, and the insertion beside it of a still grander transept with an octagonal tower that the east end came to eclipse the west by the late 12th century. A trefoil east end distinguished the church of St Mary in Capitol, Cologne, on its consecration in 1069. At the end of the 12th century the trefoil form was retained for the Church of the Apostles, Cologne. The exteriors of these works, like the cathedral at Mainz, are rich in galleries, arcades, string courses, turrets and towers.

51 **Maria Laach, abbey church** 1093–1156.

In a long, but conservative, building campaign, the
formula achieved at St Michael, Hildesheim (see 41,
page 111) – with two apses, two transepts and six towers – is
perfected with the addition of an atrium and the vaulting
of the interior over a regular succession of piers with
attached shafts.

52 **Maria Laach, abbey church** interior.

53 **Tournai, cathedral** 1110 and later, from the east.

The nave, an early example of a four-story elevation (c. 1135), has piers relieved with shafts of blue stone and an external gallery at clerestory level which recalls Italian practice. A trefoil east end was added from 1165. Twin towers flanked each apse, after the manner, for example, of St-Riquier (see 14, page 45) and St Cyriakus, Gernrode (see 39

scendent majesty as much as with the threshold of the supernatural. For the Salians that threshold was still a westwork of the Carolingian type, and the original one at Speyer (see 46, page 117) is certainly not atypical in incorporating a triple portal recalling the most sumptuous triumphal arch form retained by Constantine in Rome. The Roman triumphal arch descends from the ancient twin-towered portal of epiphany. Already in late Ottonian Strassburg those towers had reasserted themselves as essential elements in the entrance to the City of God.

North Italian churches

While most of Italy from Aquileia to Apulia sustained the early Christian tradition, the Lombards continued the development of masonry and vaulting which impressed Henry IV. Their introduction of the rib to

and 40, pages 106–9), but there they are square. The eastern ones are missing as the eastern apse was replaced by an extended Gothic sanctuary in the 13th century, but the northern and southern ones, associated with the crossing lantern, provide the most spectacular surviving witness to imperial Romanesque aspiration.

54 **Milan, Sant'Ambrogio** c. 950–1050 and later, nave and sanctuary.

The church was an early Christian foundation, but the apse, crypt and subsidiary eastern sanctuaries are of the mid-10th century. Evidently the old nave survived until 1067, the new one being in use by 1093. The western bay was still incomplete even when the atrium was finished

the groin vault is marked by the nave of Sant'Ambrogio, Milan.[54] Situated between a splendid atrium and an earlier tunnel-vaulted chancel, this nave is dated to the second half of the 11th century – not without the dissent of some who would place it well after 1100 and deny its claim to primacy. Flanked by an aisle and gallery to each side, it is divided into three square bays, each twice the width of an aisle, and as the aisle bays are square they and the galleries above interpose an elevation of paired arches between the great piers of the nave. A fourth bay before the main apse, with the sanctuary over the crypt, as at Old St Peter's, has squinches and a low dome but the other three have groin vaults crossed by diagonal ribs.

Doubtless familiar with the brick skeleton of Roman concrete vaults, the Lombards would have

and the tower begun in 1123. Meanwhile, major damage was inflicted on the church by an earthquake in 1117: the vaults were repaired – or built – thereafter. The vaults of S Nazaro, Milan (formerly the Church of the Holy Apostles, begun 382) may be earlier, but it is also possible that primacy belonged to some other work destroyed by the earthquake.

55 **Parma, cathedral and baptistry** cathedral dedicated
in 1006, substantially rebuilt after an earthquake in 1117
but vaulted only after 1162; the baptistry is of 1196.

The façade of the cathedral represents an enrichment of
the formula developed in Lombardy: the broad gable and its
stepped gallery rise from a massive wall pierced by two
horizontal galleries and a portico still recalling the central
motive (at least) of the Palace of the Exarch, Ravenna– and
the Carolingian westwork. The columns of the portal are

found that the construction of a permanent centring across the diagonals of each bay facilitated the laying of the vault and they may well have believed that ribs provided necessary reinforcement where two membranes of vaulting met in large-scale constructions. But their purpose was at least as much aesthetic: doubtless inspired by Muslim practice (see volume 6, FOUR CALIPHATES, pages 97–111), they revealed the ribs to articulate structure at the salient line of intersection of each segment of vaulting and to bind the lateral arches of each bay into a completely integrated skeletal frame.

The precedent set at Sant'Ambrogio – if a precedent it was – was followed across northern Italy to Parma.[55] The basilica there was complemented by a magnificent campanile, free-standing in the Lombard tradition, and an unexcelled baptistry. That complex was rivalled perhaps only at Florence and Pisa. The bap-

characteristically carried on the backs of lions. Inside, instead of the alternating rhythm of major and minor piers, as in Sant'Ambrogio, Milan (see 54, page 128), a regular succession of piers sustains triforium gallery and clerestory. The colonnaded galleries that distinguish the exterior of the octagonal baptistry recur inside.

56 PREVIOUS PAGES **Pisa, baptistry, cathedral and tower** 1063–1272.

Celebrating a naval triumph over the Saracens in 1062, the cathedral was consecrated in 1118. The 13th-century façade, a direct expression of the basilican volume with tiers of elegant arcades probably anticipated before the nave's extension in the second half of the 13th century, represents the formula used widely in west-central Italy. The transepts are hardly less than additional basilicas perpendicular to the main east–west one, and their conjunction recalls the great cruciform shrine of St Simeon, Qal'at Si'man (c. 476–90) in Syria – the Pisans transported Crusaders to the Holy Land from the end of the 11th century.

The baptistry may derive from the Anastasis rotunda in Jerusalem (see 96, page 207), which enclosed the sepulchre from which Christ supposedly had risen and was variously covered by a conical and domical vault – both combined at Pisa. The arcading of the tower is consistent in style and date with the west front of the cathedral, and was continued – suitably adjusted – even after subsidence initiated the lean.

57 **Pisa, cathedral** interior.

The regular rhythm of the nave colonnade is unbroken before the larger arch of the transept.

58 **Florence, S Miniato al Monte** 1062, interior.

The Roman basilican formula is sustained without transepts and the columns are modelled on Roman ones – if they are not actually antique survivors. The geometrical patterning of the two-toned marble revetment was to remain popular in the area well into the Renaissance.

59 **Modena, cathedral** nave to sanctuary.

The cathedral was founded in 1099 by Matilda of Canossa who was also a patron of S Miniato al Monte's.

tistry alone remains from the early Christian context at Florence (see volume 4, IMPERIAL SPACE, page 236), but the splendid triad at Pisa is marred only by the tilt to its tower.[56] The basilica is exceptionally grand and varicoloured in its internal revetment, like many Italian works, but continuation of the nave arcading across the transepts is more common in the Byzantine east (see volume 4, IMPERIAL SPACE, page 181).[57]

On the other hand, in the contemporary Florentine S Miniato al Monte (see volume 4, IMPERIAL SPACE, page 238), diaphragm arches carried on piers of four addorsed half-columns define three compartments, the innermost one raised as the chancel over a crypt.[58] Diaphragm arches, originally supporting a wooden roof, an alternating rhythm and raised chancel are all features of the cathedral at Modena, but apart from inserting a transept, the builders added a floor-less

60 **Verona, S Zeno Maggiore** founded c. 1030, mainly built between 1123 and 1138, nave to sanctuary raised over the crypt.

The absence of galleries below the clerestory is common in Italy; so too is the wooden roof, which here has an early Gothic trefoil profile.

61 **Padua, Sant'Antonio** exterior.

62 **Padua, Sant'Antonio** interior.

Distinct from the Greek-cross formula perfected for
S Marco, Venice, a Latin cross arrangement of seven domed
spaces was provided to cope with the volume of pilgrims
to the extremely popular shrine of St Anthony.

gallery to the interior and an inaccessible one to the exterior in exceptional preference of form over function.[59] Without gallery or diaphragm arches, the alternating rhythm recurs most impressively in S Zeno Maggiore, Verona.[60] To the east, the Venetians were still building S Marco in homage to the Byzantine quincunx with its revetment of ethereal mosaics (see volume 4, IMPERIAL SPACE, pages 243–246) and developing its formula at Padua in the 13th century.[61–62]

By the mid-10th century the most virile power in the west was Normandy and the support of its duke was crucial to the elevation of Hugh Capet in place of the Carolingian kings. For two centuries his descendants fought to extend the royal domain beyond the area later known as Ile-de-France, centred on Paris, and to re-assert central control by exploiting divisions among the magnates. They succeeded in Champagne, but Capet had been given the crown because he was thought to be the weakest of the contenders. His dynasty's ambition naturally turned supporters into opponents and the Normans effectively frustrated it for two centuries. The details of French feudal rivalry are beyond this book, except in so far as they prompted the transformation of the castle and ensured that within the overall unity of the massive round-arched Romanesque style there was much greater diversity of approach to the planning and detailing of the church than in the German empire. There was, however, one major – if indirect – consequence of feudal rivalry.

The crusades

In November 1095, at Clermont-Ferrand in the Massifs of south-central France, the French pope, Urban II

(1088–99), an enthusiastic reformer, called for the energies of militant feudalism to be directed to the penance of a crusade to recover the Holy Land. Cleansing the church of licentiousness and venality, defending it from lay interference, stamping out heresy, asserting infallibility, the successors of Leo IX were bound to turn their attention to reclaiming jurisdiction over the holiest of Christian places, the scenes of Christ's Passion lost to Christendom by the incompetent Byzantines whose heretical church Rome had finally rejected. This was a God-fearing age at its apex but the spiritual mission had material purpose too: the population was expanding – including the ranks of lordly younger sons looking for opportunity – and economic growth in much of western Europe was at a level unequalled since the fall of the Roman empire, releasing great energy despite the dissipation of a feudal age; castles were still rude but the church was increasingly sumptuous – especially in Cluniac domains – and Italian merchants in particular wanted to recover access to the luxuries of the east lost to the Muslims.

The emperor Henry IV was in no mood to support the further advance of papal power and prestige, but the French and Normans were enthusiastic. The problems of organisation and transport, of leadership and coordination with the eastern emperor Alexios I (1081–1118) were far from fully resolved when the first of four contingents of crusaders, led by the brother of the Capetian king Philip I (1060–1108), set off in August 1096. Some went overland, others by sea on ships provided by Italian maritime republics such as Pisa. After great vicissitude on all sides Jerusalem fell in July 1099 and a Latin kingdom was established in Palestine. There were to be many more crusades to protect and sustain it.

The castle

In response to the Viking incursions that decisively weakened central power under the later Carolingians, French magnates built the greatest concentration of castles in western Europe in the 10th century, but there are few remains earlier than the 11th century. Developing the defensive arrangement of a series of obstacles along a naturally secure site and providing a succession of retreats to the ultimate sanctum of a tower, walls were of earth and timber until stone was introduced in the late 10th century, as for the main walls at Chinon (see 7, pages 18–19) and the

63 **Langeais, castle** late 10th century, keep.

Dominated by the earliest significant example of a rectangular stone keep enclosing a great hall, as distinct from a tower with strictly limited accommodation, the first castle at Langeais was built by 995. The keep was c. 16 by 7 metres (52 by 23 feet); the masonry of its surviving east and north sides is rough, but regularly coursed. The hall, raised over service quarters and entered from a stair-turret, had a timber floor and roof.

precocious rectangular keep enclosing a great hall at Langeais.[63] Loches is among Langeais' most impressive early followers.[64]

Perched on a crag cut off from a chain of hills at the confluence of the Cher and Loire, Chinon is a textbook example of the defensive castle: across the ravine separating the crag from the neighbouring outcrop of rock, three wards are separated by deep trenches traversable only by a drawbridge. The zone of last resort, the Château du Coudray, was founded in the 10th century but transformed at various reprises after the mid-12th century. Then circular multifoil and polygonal forms were preferred for keeps and for the towers set at intervals around

The castle's lord was Fulk Nerra, who succeeded to the county of Anjou in 987 and pursued a notoriously brutal career until his death in 1040. Its main purpose was to overawe Tours and keep at bay Nerra's principal rivals, the counts of Blois. Both counties had belonged to Robert the Strong, ancestor of the Capetians, but with the elevation of his descendant, Hugh, to the duchy of the Franks they were entrusted to viscounts who soon assumed the title of count in nominal vassalage to the king.

64 **Loches** keep.

The site was fortified in Merovingian times, but its surviving stone keep (c. 24 by 14 metres/80 by 45 feet and originally c. 40 metres/130 feet high) was begun late in the career of Nerra and finished, with its shorter rectangular projection to the north for access, in the late 11th century. If not the rectangular form of the main volume and its adjunct, the splendid ashlar masonry, relieved with semi-cylindrical shafts, demonstrates considerable advance over the work at Langeais (see 63, page 146). Over service rooms at ground level, halls with wooden floors and roofs were superimposed on three storeys. The ring walls with their towers built over a semi-parabolic plan were begun in the late 12th century.

perimeter walls because they provided less cover for the enemy than protruding corners and their greater cohesiveness made it more difficult for sappers and miners to bring them down.

The advantage of circular forms seems to have been realised by Europeans first in Spain after Christian forces acquired Muslim strongholds built in accordance with a tradition that goes back through Abbasid Samarra at least to the Umayyad Qasr al-Hayr al-Sharqi in Syria (see volume 6, FOUR CALIPHATES, page 42).[65] The rectangular keep appears first, perhaps, on the edge of Castile – at Covarrubias c. 950, for instance – and many captured qasrs were endowed with one, but cylindrical towers punctuate the walls of Avila erected over the decade from 1090. The extended series of curved towers projecting from the stone walls there was unprecedented in Europe – if not the Middle East – since Roman antiquity (see volume 4, IMPERIAL SPACE, page 12). Indeed, built to protect a base for the troops of Castile in the aftermath of the conquest of Toledo in 1085 and therefore far more extensive than the perimeter of a castle, Avila's defences were probably Roman in origin, but the site in territory disputed by Christians and Muslims had long

65 **Montealegre** 11th century, but restored on earlier foundations, alcázar.

The plan is trapezoidal rather than rectangular as is more usual in the Arabic tradition, but the regular disposition of square or round towers to each side is typical of the form brought to Spain from Syria by the Umayyads in the 8th century.

been desolate. Stone had not been used so extensively for fortification in the west since the fall of Rome, and Avila stands at the head of a great line of walled cities that developed with the revival of urban economy from the late 12th century.

Meanwhile the square stone tower continued to dominate feudalism in most of the rest of Europe. Henry IV's Herzburg (see 37–38, pages 102–103) may be seen as the culmination of a great spate of stone tower building in central Europe.[66–67] Crusader work in the Holy Land has already been encountered at Saône (see 5, page 16) where the construction of the great, square stone keep was probably begun in the early 12th century when the Latins supplanted the Byzantines in the expansion of the principality of Antioch. The splendid Norman contribution to the development of the

66 Lake Geneva, Chillon castle late 10th century.

The dominant element in the centre of the castle is the Tour d'Alinge. Probably begun about the same time as Nerra's work at Langeais (see 63, page 146), it is not yet a keep of that capacity, but is rather more than a watchtower. The extensive range of subsidiary towers and curtain walls was developed over several centuries.

67 **Salzburg, Festung Hohensalzburg.**

One of a chain of fortresses dominating passes through the Alps, the original tower at the heart of the complex was founded in the papal cause in 1077, the year of Henry IV's submission to Gregory VII at Canossa. As usual, the rest of the site was developed over several centuries. The civil war provoked by the investiture dispute, furthering the feudal decentralisation of power, naturally led to the proliferation of castles which had been strictly controlled by Henry's predecessors.

castle, especially in England, will be encountered in due course.

The church

Though feudal regionalism was manifest in distinct schools of Romanesque architecture in the lands that would be France, the extended arteries of the pilgrimage routes and the extensive network of relationships between the monasteries – especially the imperial system of the Benedictines ruled from Cluny – ensured that no single approach was long confined to a particular region. And after the settlement of the Normans, relief released great reconstructive energy. As elsewhere, there were two broad phases that may be represented by Cluny II and III in the heart of Burgundy, at the crossroads of communication: with the Loire and the west, the Rhône and the south, the Saône and the north-east – that is, with west-central France where there was innovative planning, with Lombard Italy where there was technological development, and with the empire where there was munificent patronage.

Cluniac building

Cluny II, begun c. 950 after Hungarian raids had devastated the area, was completed in the early 11th century. As the order's magnificence reached its apogee in the last quarter of that century, it was superseded with an entirely new and definitive church, known as Cluny III, built to its north, but its sanctuary was retained for special conclaves and its narthex was incorporated in the abbot's palace to either side of the enlarged cloister.[68] In its turn Cluny III, the largest of medieval

68 **Cluny III, monastery** c. 1150, plan.

(1) New church; (2) entrance to monastic forecourt; (3) sanctuary of Cluny II adapted as the scene of special conclaves adjacent to chapter house; (4) narthex of Cluny II adapted as the court of the abbot's palace; (5) cloister; (6) dormitories; (7) refectory; (8) novices' cloister; (9) infirmary; (10) lady chapel.

Under Abbot Hugh of Semur, elected in 1049, the number of monks at Cluny grew from c. 70 to 200 by 1085, and a corresponding expansion of accommodation was needed. Comparison with Cluny II (see 21, page 66) clearly reveals the extent of the work that developed over 70 years.

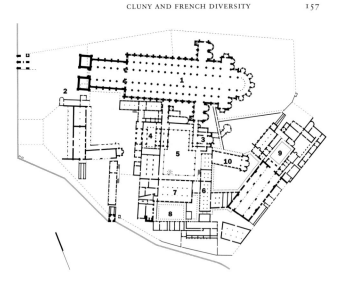

churches, succumbed to early 19th-century vandalism, except for a transept and fragments of its westwork,[69] but the plan has been reconstructed from the foundations, internal and external elevations from descriptions, documents and the surviving elements.

St-Philibert, Tournus, goes some way to compensate for the loss of Cluny – especially Cluny II. Fleeing Deas in 856, where they had sought to escape the Normans and developed an ambulatory in their new church, the monks of St-Philibert-de-Grandlieu settled in 875 by the river Saône just north of Cluny's future site. Devastated again in 937 by the Hungarians, they rebuilt after 950 and this time planned for stone vaults.

A generation earlier, Cluny II (see 21, page 66) retained parallel apses at its east end, but the relics of St Philibert were enshrined in a crypt with a semicircular ambulatory and radiating chapels which were repeated at ground level beyond the sanctuary apse – after the example set for St Martin, Tours (see 28, page 77). As at Cluny, the nave joined a long transept with a central tower and a twin-towered westwork with a chapel over a narthex. At Cluny, the nave had its regular tun-

69 **Cluny III, remaining south transept** from the west.

70 **Tournus, St-Philibert** sanctuary dedicated 1019, nave vaulting begun 1066.

nel vault by 1010. At about the same time, vaulting began at Tournus with groins in the aisles and narthex, and regular tunnels over the sanctuary, transept and westwork chapel – the latter with pilaster strips in the Lombard manner and transverse arches.[70] However, from c. 1066 each nave bay was given a transverse tunnel, admitting more light through larger clerestory windows than the normal form at Cluny.

Begun in 1088, dedicated in 1130, Cluny III was the product of more than a century of imperial expansion and increasing wealth brought to its apogee by the commanding Hugh of Semur, abbot for 60 years from 1049 and one of history's greatest patrons of architecture. It was equally the product of the elaboration of music, mastery of stone carving, and development – ultimately at Hugh's volition – of the evermore substantial basilica with chevet, towered transepts, tunnel-vaulted naves with transverse arches, complex piers, galleries and clerestories, groin-vaulted aisles, and twin-towered westworks. The influence of St Martin, Tours (see 28, page 77), fundamental here as elsewhere, was channelled most directly through St-Benoît-sur-Loire[71–73] with its substantial narthex and two transepts, both without aisles, as at Cluny II.

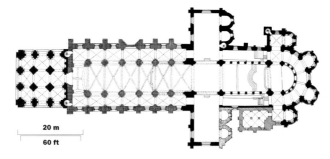

71 **St-Benoît-sur-Loire** c. 1080–1130, plan.

Founded c. 673 to enshrine the bones of St Benedict, brought to the Loire valley after the desecration of Monte Cassino by the Lombards, the abbey church was rebuilt to cater for the growth of pilgrimage to the site in the last quarter of the 11th century. A dedication ceremony was held in 1108, but construction is thought to have continued for another generation.

72 St-Benoît-sur-Loire from the west.

Over the narthex, the westwork is a development of the
form of tower attached to the west end of the original
church of St Martin, Tours (see 28, page 77) rather than of the
arrangement at St-Riquier (see 14, page 45). The westwork
contains a chapel of St Michael, but it lost its upper stages in
the 16th century.

Designed to accommodate the whole brotherhood of the order, however, Cluny III's scale was unprecedented: the main body, preceded by a westwork rising over a narthex longer than its predecessor's nave and flanked by double aisles, was c. 160 metres (525 feet) long and rose to c. 30 metres (98 feet) through triforium and clerestory to the apex of its pointed tunnel vault.[74-75] Appearing north of the Alps for the first time on such a scale, the pointed arch seems to have come from Sicily via Monte Cassino where the Islamic tradition was sustained by the Christians (see volume 4, IMPERIAL SPACE, page 235), and much else of ori-

73 **St-Benoît-sur-Loire** nave to sanctuary.

Flanked by groin-vaulted aisles, the nave originally had a wooden roof over a clerestory but no triforium. The arcades are carried on piers with attached columns (the main ones cut off from the base). The lines of nave and aisles are continued beyond the transept to form the tunnel-vaulted sanctuary, but the piers are replaced by columns. The crossing has a lantern tower after the precedent set for St Martin, Tours (see 28, page 77). A second transept separates the sanctuary from the apse and the ambulatory with its four radiating chapels.

ental derivation was manifest in the decorative detail – not least the cusped arches of the triforium. Yet the capitals of the pilasters and half columns which articulated the great piers of the nave re-evoked the classical Corinthian. Elsewhere, particularly on the columns screening the sanctuary from the ambulatory, classical stylisation was superseded by Christian didacticism.

The accumulation of chapels around the ambulatory was anticipated at St Martin, Tours (see 28, page 77), of course, though the accumulation of towers was positively imperial, as was the repetition of transepts.[76] However, the combination of all these with the discipline of consistent modules and semi-centralised, essentially centrifugal, planning about the crossing tower – except to the west where verticality is brusquely superseded by extreme basilical horizontality – generated a mass equalled in majesty only by Hagia Sophia (Church of the Holy Wisdom), Constantinople (see volume 4, IMPERIAL SPACE, pages 208–215). As in Byzantium, the Pantokrator dominated the interior, but from the main apse rather than a central dome.

Apart from the surviving transept (see 69, page 158),

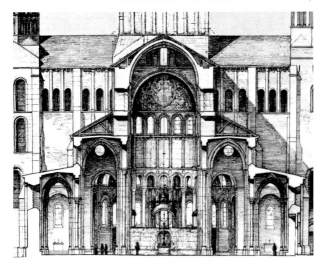

74 **Cluny III, monastery** transverse section.

75 Cluny III begun 1088, mainly complete by 1121, reconstruction of nave.

Built on a plan defined in harmony with a modular system inspired by Vitruvian symmetry, and celebrated for its acoustics, the great church extended to 11 bays before the first of two transepts, and two more before the second transept. The ambulatory was screened from the apse by a semicircle of columns, but the rest of the main arcade was carried on recessed piers with attached columns. The aisles were doubled, as at Tours (at least after 1050). Except in the apse, there were both triforium and clerestory throughout and an additional zone of clerestory lighting above the inner aisles produced a four-storey elevation to the narthex (c. 1122). The tunnel vaults over the nave and the transverse arches between the groin-vaulted bays of the aisles were pointed in profile to reduce the thrust. Nevertheless, part of the vault collapsed in 1125 and heavy quadrant arches – putative flying buttresses – were projected out from the clerestory to transmit the thrust of the vault to the piers between the aisles. The first of these buttresses may have been inserted in the early 1130s when the construction of the narthex was begun: as the exercise continued into the next century it may have followed the Gothic lead rather than anticipating it.

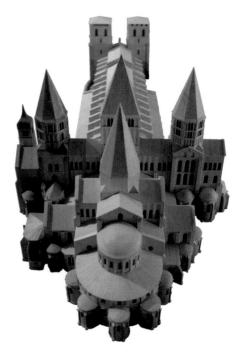

77 **Nevers, St-Etienne** after 1083, east end with the ambulatory.

Lucid in plan, meticulous in its masonry, St-Etienne marks the maturity of the Cluniac style on the reduced scale of a dependent abbey. Single aisles flank the barrel-vaulted nave; there is a single barrel-vaulted transept before the sanctuary and ambulatory, but there are galleries and a clerestory throughout. The three original towers were reduced after the French Revolution.

76 **Cluny III** block model (Cluny Abbey Museum).

some idea of the greatness of Cluny III's loss is conveyed by the best of contemporary Cluniac priory churches: St-Etienne, Nevers,[77] begun just before St Hugh's great church, and Notre-Dame, Paray-le-Monial.[78] The cathedral of St-Lazare, Autun is also indispensable to the reconstructed image.[79] Disparate in style, the abbey church of Ste-Madeleine, Vézelay

78 PREVIOUS PAGES Paray-le-Monial, Notre-Dame c. 1110.

The church is a reduced version of the Cluny III model (see 76, page 170), though less complex in plan and mass. The interior elevation is most directly derived from the model.

79 Autun, St-Lazare c. 1120, nave.

The nave is another close follower of Cluny III, but in the absence of an ambulatory three tiers of windows light the apse. Whereas the three-bay clerestory echoes the triforium in Cluny III and Paray-le-Monial, in the nave each clerestory bay has only a single light. Instead of shaft-like half columns, the piers are articulated with pilasters which approximate classical proportions. However, they support superb didactic capitals rather than Corinthian acanthus foliage.

80 **Vézelay, Ste-Madeleine** 1096–1137, narthex.

An essential element in the formula transmitted from St-Benoît-sur-Loire (see 73, page 164), the narthex was begun before the one on Cluny III. It shelters a portal which, opening to the nave under the Pantokrator as the porta coeli, is one of the chief glories of medieval France.

81 **Vézelay, Ste-Madeleine** nave.

Built in place of its burnt Carolingian predecessor, the nave does not conform to the Cluniac formula: there is no triforium except in the later apse, and the groin-vaulted bays are separated by bold transverse arches of varicoloured masonry. There is, however, a classicising tendency in the proportions and detail of the attached columns from which the nave arcade springs.

marks the further development of substituting groin vaults for the tunnel over the nave:[80-81] ribbed and in combination with the pointed arch and flying buttresses of Cluny III, they provided the key to the future.

Cistercian austerity

The spiritual revival of the late 11th century – the age of zealous popes and humiliated emperors – promoted wide-ranging reform within the Christian establishment which certainly did not fail to affect Cluny's empire. Several new orders emerged from dissatisfaction with manifest luxury and perceived laxity within the Benedictine world in the contrary conviction that the best way to God was through humility and self-denial. One band of monks dedicated anew to St Benedict's original ideal left the abbey of Molesme in 1098 to establish a severely ascetic rule at Cîteaux: manual labour was reintroduced for all, feudal endowments were rejected and absolute simplicity of liturgy was reflected in the uncompromising austerity of building. This Cistercian Order spread particularly rapidly after the young brother Bernard was sent out from Cîteaux to found a new house at Clairvaux in 1115. Under his direction, the process was repeated many times, but the central ideal was not diluted: each new house was dependent on the one from which it was founded, all were to subscribe to precisely the same rule, each was to be visited annually by the abbot of its founding house and all the abbots were to meet annually at Cîteaux.

St Bernard (1090–1153) was profoundly influenced by St Augustine, his theology of number and his discovery of the key to the City of God in musical harmony (see 9, page 22). In the consonance of music St Bernard heard ultimate truth and his notorious puritanism was bent to the moulding of a context in which no other sensory delight would interfere with the apprehension of that truth through sound – except the inner eye of the soul attuned to harmony which would see the translation of those aural consonances into the perfect proportions and pure geometry of the church itself. He rejected the grand scale and sumptuous ornament of Cluny as inconsistent with the humility proper to the monk, but the bizarre representationalism of Cluniac sculpture was not condemned out of hand: except perhaps for the expense, it was admissible to resort to material imagery for the instruction of the laity seduced by the things of this world, but it was a distracting irrelevance to the aspiration of the monk to spiritual vision into the ultimate truth of the City of God. Thus, it is hardly surprising that the perfect ratios derived by St Augustine from the Pythagorean *tetractys* inform all the parts of a Cistercian church such as the abbey of Fontenay in central France – which St Bernard may well have designed.[82]

82 **Fontenay** 1139–47, plan.
  (1) Church; (2) chapter house; (3) dormitory;
(4) refectory; (5) fountain; (6) workshops.
  Facilities for outsiders were strictly limited and were confined to the west gate. In the design and construction of their abbeys, as in all else, the Cistercians aimed at self-sufficiency.
  The main ratios are 1:1 for the façade and the essentially cubical bays of nave and aisles below the springing of the vaults; 1:2 for the width of aisles to nave, for the length of transept to nave, for the width and length of the transept and for the height of the aisle arcade to the internal elevation of the nave wall; 2:3 for the width of the sanctuary to its total length including the crossing; 3:4 for the width of the nave plus aisles to the length of the transept.

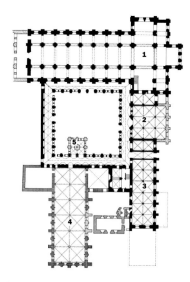

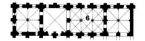

83 **Fontenay** interior.

84 **Sénanque** refectory.

85 **Sénanque** founded 1148.

In contrast with Benedictine display, Cistercian austerity is nowhere better represented than at Fontenay,[83] though it was common to all the houses of the uniformitarian order. It was imposed by standardised planning derived from Benedict of Aniane's blueprint (see 20, page 62) as well as St Augustine's geometry, but remoteness of site was preferred and topography often dictated deviation. Sculpture was proscribed in the early life of the order and without a towered façade, ambulatory or crypt, generally rectangular in plan, the church relied for aesthetic effect solely on the regular repetition of arches – but these were invariably pointed like those of Cluny III (see 74, page 167). Certainly no less austere were the main buildings around the cloister – which might be to the south or the north of the church, as the site determined – the vaulted chapter house, the dormitory accessible directly from the church, the refectory perpendicular to the cloister range opposite the church.[84, 85]

Regional variety

Such austerity was unique to the Cistercians but re-
evoked classicism was not confined to Burgundy. Certainly it was at its richest where the abbots of Cluny
maintained that all the resources of art should be
employed for the glory of God, but it was hardly less
rich in Provence, itself exceptionally rich in Roman
remains. Insecurity of dating has left ultimate responsibility for the revival of Roman ornament unclear.
Because of its heritage, Provence might well seem the
most obvious source, but the best examples are generally thought to post-date the conception of Cluny III.
The triumphal portal of St-Trophîme, Arles,[86] for
example, has been placed in the 1170s, at the earliest,
when the nave was rebuilt, and the even more sumptuous three-arched version at St-Gilles-du-Gard is possibly a generation earlier. In Provence, as elsewhere,
classicism was transformed with didactic decorative
detail: portals apart, this is especially striking in the
wide variety of capitals in cloister colonnades which
typically present immediately appreciable images of
the wages of sin.[87]

Beyond varied approaches to ornament, French
Romanesque admitted no less variety of plan, space

86 **Arles, St-Trophîme** c. 1180, façade.

In the synthesis of triumphal arch and temple front, no less than in the proportions of the columns, classicism is honoured in the breach rather than in full faith – despite the abundance of models in close proximity.

The façade of the priory church of St-Gilles-du-Gard is assigned to the mid-12th century – at least in inception. On the other hand, the relatively austere portal of Notre-Dame-des-Domes, Avignon has been dated to c. 1200, though the aisleless nave is earlier.

87 **Arles, St-Trophîme** cloister range.

The stout corner piers, providing support for the quadrant vaults, have fluted pilasters and figures in high relief. The arches of the intermediate bays spring from a variety of circular and octagonal shafts with a spectacular set of didactic and Corinthianesque capitals.

and mass, and though distinct regional preferences may be discerned, they are far from absolute. St-Trophîme, Arles and St-Gilles-du-Gard are basilican but many Provençal churches are aisleless like Notre-Dame-des-Domes, Avignon: the form derives from the unobstructed space of the antique audience hall or council chamber – the basic basilica as 'the place of the king' (see volumes 3, IMPERIAL FORM, page 147, and 4, IMPERIAL SPACE, page 31). And the two types, the single volume and the composite, were developed in parallel – even cross-fertilised – elsewhere, most notably in western France.

The aisled basilica is certainly the most common form throughout France, as almost everywhere else with or without stone vaulting, though no one alternative arrangement was the preserve of any one area. The ambulatory with radiating chapels predominates after Cluny III but does not entirely supplant parallel apses. Some form of westwork is normal, usually with twin towers as at Cluny III, often with one, occasionally with three. Internal elevations vary too, but not in accordance with any regional pattern: the aisles may be lower than the nave, permitting a two-storey elevation with clerestory as in the early Christian form –

and as at St-Benoît-sur-Loire or Ste-Madeleine, Véze-lay (see 73 and 80, pages 164 and 176). They may support a gallery, as at St Martin, Tours (see 28, page 78), and they may be surmounted by both gallery and clerestory, as at Cluny III or St-Lazare, Autun (see 75 and 79, pages 169 and 175) and in the great churches of the Capetian domain where aspiration in building matched imperial pretension.[88]

The influence of Cluny III was as widespread as its network of priories, but its formula was used or varied more widely still. Nowhere is this better illustrated, perhaps, than in neighbouring Auvergne – though the influence of the Loire, which helped mould Cluny III, had already affected the mid-10th century architects of the cathedral at Clermont-Ferrand. That work has

88 **Reims, St-Remi** begun 1005, 13th-century vaults reconstructed in the 20th century, nave.

The first church enshrining the tomb of St Remigius, the baptist of Clovis I, was consecrated 852. A grander new one was built between 1005 and 1034 in response to the great popularity of pilgrimage to the site. Its three-storey internal elevation, with wide, light arches to aisles and galleries, supported a flat wooden roof over the exceptionally broad

nave. Narrow aisles around the transepts led to a sanctuary
with parallel apses, and later in the century an ambulatory
with radiating chapels was built around the main sanctuary
apse, completing the church's concordance with the
pilgrimage type defined for St Martin, Tours (see 28, page 77).
Later still, the wooden roof was replaced with rib vaults,
despite the great width of the main spaces, and the
substantial mass of wall above the triforium was relieved
with blind pointed arches.

The stone vault had obvious advantages of durability but
limitations of scale, as structural technology in the period of
its inception restricted the height, width and lightness of
naves. Thus, until well into the 11th century the wooden
roof was usually preferred because it was easier and cheaper
to construct and because it allowed a lighter structure to the
body of the church and wider spans to the main spaces,
especially in the north where light was at a premium and
where the danger of raids and destruction by fire was less
acute in great centres remote from coasts, like Chartres or
Reims. Both these considerations – the vulnerability of
timber, the limitation of space – ensured that most of the
greatest mature Romanesque churches of the French
monarchy's heartland have disappeared. St-Remi is perhaps
the main exception.

long been obscured, but its influence, the influence of Cluny III, of Islam – or the Mozarabic transmitted by pilgrims returning from Santiago de Compostela – and local idiosyncrasy are all well represented by Notre-Dame-du-Port, Clermont-Ferrand[89] and many churches in settlements around the metropolis, like St-Austremoine, Orcival.[90]

In a cross between our two types of basilica, aisles and nave may match in height though not usually in width or vaulting technique: the subdivision of a vol-

89 OVERLEAF **Clermont-Ferrand, Notre-Dame-du-Port** early 12th century, nave towards the sanctuary.

Flanked by aisles and triforium gallery but no clerestory, like St Martin, Tours (see 28, page 77), the four-bay, tunnel-vaulted nave is exceptionally dark. On the other hand, light enters through and above the ambulatory around the apse, and the raising of the transept bays adjacent to the crossing tower for the insertion of clerestory windows is exceptionally dramatic. The cusped arches of the gallery echo the oriental influence detected earlier at Cluny III. The crypt under the apse and ambulatory follows the precedent set nearly two centuries earlier in the nearby cathedral, which followed the precedent set for St Martin itself.

90 **Orcival, St-Austremoine** early 12th century, from the east.

Typical of the Auvergnat churches related to Notre-Dame-du-Port, Clermont-Ferrand (see 89, page 194), the effect on the external massing of raising the transept bays next to the crossing tower is hardly less dramatic than its admission of clerestory light to the interior.

umetric entity is preferred to the accretion of distinct elements. The elimination of clerestory and gallery and the substitution of comparatively light colonnades for much weighty masonry was popular in north Aquitanian Poitou where architects seem to have been interested in spatial integrity but not necessarily in preserving it absolutely – as in Provence. Alternative arrangements are represented by the abbey church at St-Savin-sur-Gartempe, with its great colonnades and splendidly frescoed tunnel vault over the nave,[91] and at Notre-Dame-la-Grande, Poitiers[92] with its articulated piers and pointed arches. The latter also best represents its area's predilection for the rich decoration of façades, classical in inspiration if not in effect.

Further south, in the Saintonge region of central Aquitaine, many churches are almost equally as rich in ornament as the Poitevan ones and their spaces are similarly subdivided – as in St-Pierre, Aulnay and, at least in so far as external embellishment is concerned, St-Hilaire, Melle. However, from Fontevrault (well to

91 **St-Savin-sur-Gartempe** late 11th century, interior.

The apse is dated to the mid-11th century, but the nave was completed c. 1115.

92 **Poitiers, Notre-Dame-la-Grande** first half of 12th century, façade.

Rather than a free-standing commemorative arch, the façade's superimposed arcades recall a Roman triumphal city gate like the Porta dei Borsari, Verona (see volume 3, IMPERIAL FORM, page 232) or its many northern equivalents, but it is inhabited by an even richer panoply of

the north near the Loire) to Agen (well to the south on the Garonne), the most distinctive Aquitanian solution to the problem of preserving uninterrupted space depends on the pendentive dome.

A single dome over the shrine of St-Front, Périgueux[93-94] seems to have initiated the development not only of the great church there but also of an extended process in which domed spaces were aligned longitudinally or combined to form Greek and Latin crosses – with or without knowledge of the main masterpieces of the Byzantine tradition but certainly in the recognition of the self-buttressing potential of a series of domes. S Marco, Venice (see volume 4, IMPERIAL SPACE, page 245) was doubtless well enough known even in Aquitaine, so too perhaps Sicily where the Byzantine tradition was well established, and

figures – despite the absence of the tympanum usual in the main portal – and pointed arches join semicircular ones. The clustered colonnettes of the turrets and the fish-scale masonry of their conical tops is typical of the region. Inside, except in the ambulatory, the monumental cylindrical columns of St-Savin-sur-Gartempe (see 91, page 196) are supplanted by clustered piers.

93 Périgueux, St-Front plan.

A 10th-century basilica enshrining the remains of St Front was apparently given a dome before the mid-11th century, but it was burnt c. 1120. The nave walls were retained for the atrium of a vast new church begun soon after the fire, and the base of its crossing tower, raised through three stages of superimposed arcades, formed the porch. The domed sanctuary containing the saint's tomb was rebuilt on a grander scale. The main axis was continued with two similar domed chambers to the east (forming an exceptionally oriented nave as the sanctuary was retained in its original position) and two more domes were added on the cross axis. If the longitudinal alignment of domes is not uncommon in the naves of western France, the Greek cross plan of St-Front is unique in the degree of its homage to the east – in particular to the Church of the Holy Apostles, Constantinople (c. 536–50), built by Constantine, rebuilt by Justinian, which provided the model for S Marco, Venice. The position of the high altar has been moved from west to east and back again several times. The 'restorations' perpetrated by Paul Abadie in the 19th century are generally regretted, especially in so far as they interpreted the exterior.

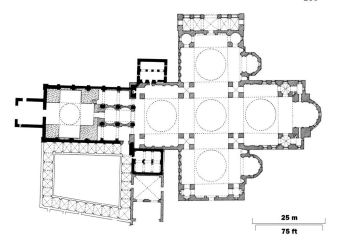

25 m
75 ft

although the first dome at St-Front is generally dated to a generation before the first crusade, the process of accumulation may well have stemmed from first-hand familiarity with Hagia Sophia, Constantinople gained on the passage to Palestine (see volume 4, IMPERIAL SPACE, page 215).

Developed over at least half a century from 1070, St-Front is the most spectacular example of a cruciform arrangement recalling S Marco. At much the same time, the alignment of two domes and a semidome with apsidal chapels radiating from it at the cathedral at Cahors (dedicated incomplete in 1119) recalls Hagia Sophia, Constantinople (see volume 4, imperial space, pages 208–215) in a primitive way, but the principle is more representatively extended at Angoulême or the abbey church at Fontevrault.[95] The latter also presents a conical variant of the dome on squinches in the centralised cluster of its splendid abbey kitchen. Perhaps the best surviving early medieval domestic building in Europe, this octagonal composition of major and minor cone-vaulted spaces may be likened to a centralised sanctuary with ambu-

94 **Périgueux, St-Front** interior.

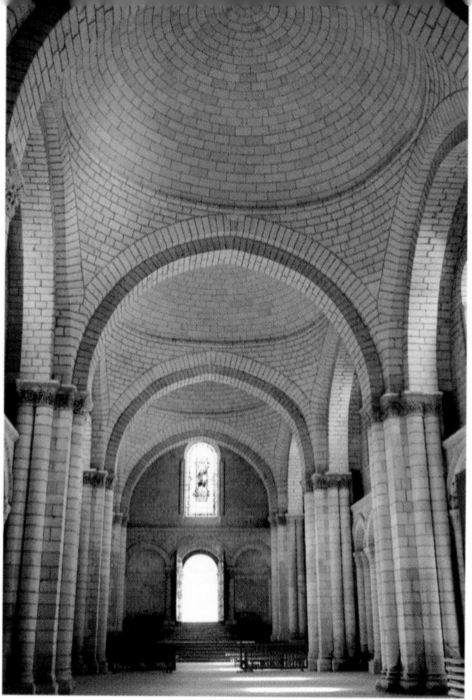

latory and radiating chapels to all sides. Aligned, two such forms provide the nave of the church of St-Ours, Loches (before 1168).

The domed church was ubiquitous. If not in Aquitaine, its Latin culmination was in Palestine in the mid-12th century with the addition of a chevet and the domed crossing of a transept to one of the most important rotundas in all Christendom, Constantine's archetypal Church of the Holy Sepulchre, Jerusalem (see volume 4, IMPERIAL SPACE, page 172).[96] That was the principal goal of pilgrims, whose security was osten-

95 **Fontevrault** c. 1120, nave towards the entrance.

The abbey was founded c. 1100 and, as the sanctuary was dedicated in 1119, the church must have been begun little more than a decade later. The nave followed over the next decade. In the vicinity of Angers, capital of Anjou, the church attracted royal patronage and was adopted by Henry II Plantagenet as the Angevin dynastic necropolis.

The four domed bays of the nave (c. 84 metres/275 feet long) were re-vaulted in the early 20th century. Earlier than the nave, the tunnel-vaulted transept has five square bays smaller than those of the nave, but commensurate with the width of the sanctuary.

96 Jerusalem, Church of the Holy Sepulchre on Golgotha 4th–12th century, plan.

The complex built under Constantine incorporated a basilica, an irregular trapezoidal court to the west and the Anastasis rotunda, enshrining the holy sepulchre, further west. During restorations carried out in the mid-11th century, the Byzantine emperor Constantine Monomachos projected chapels from an ambulatory around the rotunda. The Crusaders demolished the eastern apsidal chapel and filled the court with a new sanctuary extending to the east from the domed crossing of a transept – transept, crossing, sanctuary, apse and ambulatory in fact reproducing the arrangements developed in Europe to cater for pilgrims. A new chapel south of the new sanctuary enshrined Golgotha, the site of the crucifixion. The original basilica survived in part as the chapel of St Helena, who is reputed to have discovered the remains of the cross on the site.

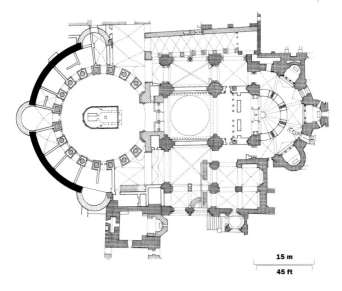

15 m
45 ft

sibly a main motive of the crusades. If there was a truly international Romanesque, it was that of the western pilgrimage church whose essential element was not the dome but the chevet – the main new form introduced by the Latins to Jerusalem.

The pilgrimage church

Pilgrimage was the main aim of international travellers and the principal destination was Rome, the seat of St Peter and the centre of Christendom after the loss of the Holy Land to the Muslims. The Alps, however, were a formidable obstacle, insurmountable to many would be pilgrims on that route. Instead, they followed the road to Santiago de Compostela, the reputed burial place of St James the Great, in north-west Spain (see 101, page 216). Along the clearly defined routes to these major cult centres, punctuated with hostels and hospices set about 30 kilometres (20 miles) apart, were secondary pilgrimage destinations with churches enshrining the remains of saints who had died in the cause of Christ or had been distinguished by the marks of divine favour.

The popularity of pilgrimage promoted important developments in church planning. Venerable remains

had usually been interred in the crypt under the sanctuary of the great church – as at Speyer (see 47, page 118)
and Santiago de Compostela (see 102, page 218) – but the
inevitably restricted confines of that situation were
inadequate to cope with the influx of ever increasing
numbers of pilgrims. The sanctuary or choir was
endowed with a ceremonial sarcophagus or statue of
the saint, ultimately in a rich shrine, and the east end
was reformed around it. After the example of St Martin, Tours, rebuilt following a fire in 997 (see 28, page 77
), the aisles were extended from the twin-towered
westwork into an unbroken circuit along the nave,
skirting the transepts, around the sanctuary through
an ambulatory with radial chapels so that the pilgrims
could make a complete tour without interrupting the
mass being celebrated.[97] In elevation, the serried ranks
of the bays were defined by composite piers, the groin-
vaulted aisles were surmounted by quadrant-vaulted
galleries but not clerestories, and tunnel vaults
replaced the original wooden roofs of nave and
transepts c. 1050.

The full realisation of the high Romanesque ideal
enshrined in the pilgrimage church, its restrained exterior articulation enhancing the direct expression of the

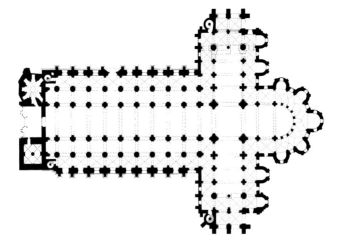

97 **Tours, St Martin** early 11th century, plan and section.
   Begun in the late 9th century, completed in the mid-11th
century, the nave had doubled aisles (like St-Bénigne, Dijon,
1001–18), but only one range continued around the
transepts to the ambulatory. It had triforium galleries, a

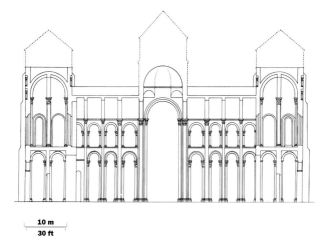

10 m
30 ft

clerestory and five towers, one at the crossing, one on each
end of the transept and a pair flanking the western portal
with rib-vaulted chambers. The east end was rebuilt from
1202. The church was destroyed after the French
Revolution.

interior, may be traced from St Martin, Tours through an example on each of the main routes to the most perfect one at the destination: St-Sernin, Toulouse,[98] begun in the 1070s; the contemporary, but much smaller, Ste-Foi, Conques;[99–100] and Santiago de Compostela, begun c. 1070 with considerable assistance from Alfonso VI of Asturias, one of Cluny's greatest patrons.[101–102]

Given Cluny's international standing, its presence in many priories tending pilgrims along the road, its responsibility for two of the principal pilgrimage churches and its indebtedness to the patron of another, it is hardly surprising that the Cluniac formula for church planning, derived through St-Benoît-sur-Loire

98 Toulouse, St-Sernin c. 1080, east end apse, ambulatory, south transept and crossing tower.

The sanctuary was consecrated in 1096 but the ambulatory was not completed until a couple of years later. The nave, the grandest of the pilgrimage series except for Santiago de Compostela (but with doubled aisles like St Martin, Tours, see 28, page 77), was substantially complete by 1120, but not yet vaulted. The west front was never completed according to the original plan.

99 **Conques, Ste-Foi** c. 1080

Construction seems to have begun with the nave, the east end followed after 1080 and the work was completed with the crossing tower c. 1130. Twin western towers were added in the 19th century either side of the magnificent Christ in Judgement portal of c. 1125.

100 **Conques, Ste-Foi** crossing and eastern bays of nave.

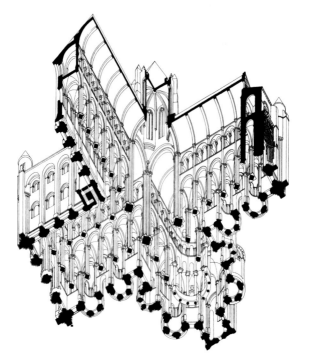

101 **Santiago de Compostela** begun c. 1075, mainly complete 1125, worm's eye axonometric (after Conant).

Set high on a terrace overlooking a splendid piazza, flanked by the archbishop's palace and a sumptuous hostel, the west front was remodelled with great bravura in the 18th century. Originally it recalled the ancient twin-towered portal of epiphany complete with the triple arch motif. Within, the narthex surmounted a substantial crypt and was surmounted by a tribune gallery as in a Carolingian westwork.

The 11-bay nave was originally screened at the tenth bay. Beyond the vast transept (of six bays to each side of the square crossing), the sanctuary is raised over the crypt containing the tomb recognised in 813 as that of the apostle. Most of the east end, within the ambulatory, is filled with a Baroque reliquary shrine, with stairs down to the crypt and up to a bridged gallery behind an effigy of the saint. The dome-like vaulting in the tower recalls the great Muslim tradition and anticipates one of the more significant developments in later Spanish medieval architecture best represented by the domical towers of the cathedral at Zamora (c. 1174).

(see 71, page 162) from old St Martin, Tours (see 28, page 77) and applied internationally, differs from the pilgrimage church type only in its unaisled transepts. It was, however, the extension of the aisle arcades around the whole perimeter of the pilgrimage church that took the Romanesque to the perfection of Santiago's fully integrated skeleton of lateral and transverse arches in which pillars, columns, colonnettes, capitals and moulded voussoirs were systematically applied to all apertures from the triumphal entrance, symbolising the threshold of Heaven, to the great bays of the nave and, ultimately, across those bays to the vaults symbolising Heaven itself. And the great tower-framed portal of St James, with its supreme representation of the Pantokrator, is the very image of the door to the

102 **Santiago de Compostela** portal.

The narthex survives behind the spectacular Baroque façade. Exposed to the west until the construction of that façade in the 18th century, the great sculpted tympanum, related to the Cluniac work at Vézelay (see 80, page 176), was executed between 1168 and 1188. It replaced an earlier Transfiguration scene, which was relocated to the south portal.

103 **Bayeux tapestry** between late 11th and mid-12th centuries, detail with a motte-and-bailey castle (Bayeux, Tapestry Museum).

A visual chronicle in wool on linen of the Norman conquest of England, this great work is associated with the circle of William the Conqueror's consort, Queen Matilda.

Traces of the mound and ward (motte-and-bailey) castles in Normandy are rare, suggesting that the conquerors developed the form – an age-old product of pragmatism – as they advanced into England. The rapidity and cost of that advance obviated the use of stone even for the tower that surmounted the motte – timber remained the norm till well into the 12th century – except for the most important works. As elsewhere, site rather than foresight determined which of the two elements came first, though in the absence of a natural hillock the mound will often have been formed of earth excavated from the ditch dug to defend the bailey.

Towards the end of the 11th century, the Normans played a major part in the crusades against the Muslims in the Holy Land. First, however, they had liberated Sicily, which had been taken from Byzantium for Islam in the 8th century. Marauding from the early 11th century, they carved domains for themselves in southern Italy, where the hold of Byzantium was fast failing, and hired themselves as mercenaries to the pope and others interested in expansion in the area. But the Normans' success established them as rivals to their employers, especially to the zealous Leo IX: their leader Robert Guiscard (c. 1015–85) was recognised as Duke of Apulia and Calabria in 1059. Shortly afterwards he and his brother, Humphrey, crossed to Sicily, and the island was wholly under Norman sway by 1091. A magnificent series of basilicas, most still early Christian in form but predominantly Lombard in style, was built along the Adriatic coast of Norman Apulia, and the new rulers of Sicily promoted a spectacularly eclectic style of architecture in which northern Romanesque grandeur was grafted on to the hybrid Byzantino-Arabic stock already flourishing there.[104] Well before Normans were kings of the south, however, they were kings in the north.

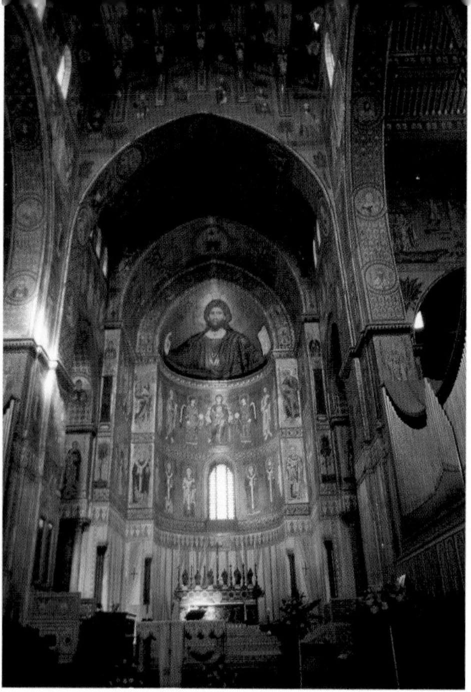

England

That Anglo-Saxon England had not entirely succumbed to the Danes in the late 9th century was due to Alfred the Great (871–99) of Wessex: having taken London he rallied the English to the offensive before he died and thus ensured that England, unlike France, emerged from the period of Viking incursions as a centralised power. His son, Edward the Elder (899–924), received the submission of most of the Danes in the east and north in 20 years of relentless combat, but it was not until his son, Athelstan (924–39), finally took Northumbria in 927 that all England was united under one king for the first time. Converted to Christianity in a revival of the church reformed along lines inspired

104 **Monreale, Sicily, Sta Maria la Nuova** 1174, nave to the sanctuary.

Though late in date, the cathedral built by William II (1154–89) marks the full flowering of the hybrid Sicilian-Norman style. The basilica is of the early Christian type with classical columns, but the east end is triapsidal like Cluny II (see 21, page 66). The pointed arches are Muslim (so too is the marble dado and the wooden ceiling), but the resplendent mosaics are Byzantine.

by Cluny, the Danes were widely accorded autonomy, but Ethelred II (978–1016) massacred many of them in face of a renewed Viking threat at the end of the century, and attracted vengeance. He fled to his brother-in-law, the Duke of Normandy, in 1013 and the English crown fell to the Danish king Canute II who became King of England (1016–35).

Canute married Ethelred's widow, Emma of Normandy, and when his son by a previous marriage died without issue in 1042, her son by Ethelred succeeded. Known as Edward the Confessor (1042–66), he too died without issue, reputedly having promised the succession to his cousin, William Duke of Normandy (1027–87), as early as 1051. By 1066, however, Edward's weak rule had seen the emergence of powerful magnates in earldoms descended from the pre-Danish Anglo-Saxon kingdoms. One of the most powerful, Godwin, Earl of Wessex, was exiled for insubordination, returned in force and had his son, Harold (c. 1020–66), confirmed as his successor in 1053. In Normandy in 1064, Harold swore to support Duke William's claim to the English throne, according to the Normans, but Edward named Harold as successor on his deathbed in January 1066.

With papal blessing for the punishment of broken oaths, William invaded, and Harold was slain at the Battle of Hastings.[103]

The Norsemen had consolidated their hold on Normandy, expanding it with the ruthless extirpation of local opposition and establishing a rigorous feudal system in which local power was delegated to viscounts based on castles. Castle-based power could be used against the centre when it was weak, as in late Carolingian France, but Normandy was ruled by a succession of strong dukes and vassalage was strictly controlled. The experience was exported to England and the Anglo-Saxons, largely undefended on their land, found themselves subjected to a conqueror who had forged an aggressive weapon from the motte-and-bailey type of fortification (see 103, page 220) – which we have encountered, in principle, with Henry the Fowler's fortified towns and their precedent in the fortified farmstead of the Dark Ages.

Although William brought feudalism, he nevertheless developed the most effectively unified state in Europe. Norman magnates replaced Anglo-Saxons as military governors but on reduced estates, and stationed in castles built by or under licence from the crown, as in Normandy. They held their position and lands in return for supplying a specified number of knights and troops to the king's army and were allowed only garrison forces themselves.

Though his successors had to compromise, William refused to recognise the claims of the reformed papacy to supremacy in England. He appointed Normans to the bishoprics and endowed them with estates on terms similar to those imposed on the secular lords. He and his successors also endowed them with a set of new cathedrals which constituted the most magnificent building exercise of its age. In England as in Normandy, moreover, abbeys were seen as keys to pacification, and the Benedictines were also magnificently endowed.

The principal officers of state were drawn from the Norman magnates, ecclesiastical and secular, but on Anglo-Saxon precedent they were summoned to regular conclave in a putative parliament and court of justice dominated by the king – and most of the Norman kings were exceptionally forceful. William was succeeded by his oldest son, Robert, in Normandy and by his second surviving son, William II (d. 1100), in England. His youngest son, Henry I (1100–35), ultimately acquired both kingdoms with the support of the Capetian king Philip I.

His son William having predeceased him, Henry I forced the English magnates to swear allegiance to his daughter, Matilda (1102–67), widow of emperor Henry V and soon to be married to Geoffrey, Count of Anjou (1113–51). In the event her cousin, Stephen of Blois (1135–54), stole the throne but her son, Henry II Plantagenet (1154–89), recovered it after a protracted conflict settled by his adoption as Stephen's heir. His was an empire in all but name: apart from England, he inherited Normandy from his mother and the usurper, Anjou and Touraine from his father and Brittany from his brother, Geoffrey. Aquitaine was added when he married its divorced heiress, Eleanor, after her repudiation by the Capetian king Louis VII (1137–80).

Norman castles

By the time of the Norman conquest of England, the castle had proliferated through fragmented France as the base for feudal power, but it was hardly known in unified England, except as a royal preserve. The type imported by the Normans had originated in the defensive establishment of the Dark Ages, but the aggressive feudatories of France, in particular, had made of it a base for the advance of power, rather than of retreat.

Not regular like the Roman camp (see volume 3, IMPERIAL FORM, page 125) but sited in open country, the Conqueror's motte-and-bailey castle was conceived to fulfil the same function of holding down the conquered. Several examples are illustrated in the Bayeux tapestry (see 103, page 220). A natural eminence was usually chosen or a mound (motte) constructed for surveillance beside a tract of ground expansive enough to accommodate the garrison (bailey). A timber tower and palisade crowned the motte, and the bailey was protected by rings of wooden posts on ramparts of impacted earth excavated from a surrounding ditch. Gradually the wooden palisades were replaced by stone walls – as at Restormel in Cornwall.[105] This, of course, is not to be mistaken as betraying a negative, defensive mentality: the walls were for protection, like the walls of a Roman camp, for hostile installations attract hostility and must be able to withstand it.

William had come over the sea and his first concern was to protect his rear: a chain of fortresses was built

105 **Restormel, castle** c. 1100 with 13th-century masonry.

The so-called shell keep replaced the timber palisade on the motte in the early 12th century at strategically important sites like Restormel, which was built to command the Fowey valley.

106 **London, White Tower** 1078, model (Bayeux, Tapestry Museum).

Like the Conqueror's castle at Winchester (early 12th century), his main seat taken over from the Saxons, the roughly rectangular stone keep of London belongs to the type represented by Fulk's Langeais (see 63, page 146) but was probably modelled on the palace built at Rouen by Fulk's Norman contemporary, Duke Richard I (942–96). Square stone towers reinforce the corners except to the south-east, where the apse of the staunch Palatine Chapel imposes a prophetic curve. The tower was entered at first-floor level from steps to the south – the basement strong rooms for

from Dover, the nearest point to France, and at strategic points along the route from there to London. Then the major lines of communication to the principal bases of power within the kingdom were similarly controlled. The Tower of London, the hub of the network, is essentially a motte-and-bailey castle: in the absence of a natural eminence at the crossing of the Thames where the Roman Londinium was sited, but using at the outset part of the old Roman city wall, a massive square tower stands for the motte in the centre of the bailey.[106] Exceptional because it was to be a seat of the king (though Winchester remained the capital), the tower was built of stone from the outset, but Norwich, Canterbury and Rochester, among others, followed its example in the reign of Henry I. To ensure all-round protection and provide for the expanding needs of the court as the Norman monarchy increased its hold on

stores (and occasional prisoners) were not accessible from the ground. The upper storeys are divided by a massive cross wall that provides internal support as well as diversification of space. The outer walls, of Kentish rag, are c. 27 metres (90 feet) high and c. 4.5 metres (15 feet) thick at the base, decreasing to c. 3.4 metres (11 feet) at the top.

England, the original single palisade around London's tower was doubled. When Henry II established his Plantagenet line, this concentric approach to the protection of major offensive establishments was to be the standard in England.

Norman churches

The Norman dukes began building – or rebuilding – within a generation of the establishment of their realm, and if the scale was modest at first, the ambition was not. Architecturally, that ambition was fed from as many sources as the long ships had reached with their Viking ancestors. The twin-towered westwork of the Rhine and the galleried internal elevation of the Loire both inspired the design of St-Pierre, Jumièges, well advanced by 950. Monastic reformers came from the orbit of Cluny at the beginning of the new century, and several new abbey churches built soon after, like at Bernay,[107] retained the parallel apses of Cluny II, though the form *en échelon* was already being superseded by the chevet of ambulatory with radiating chapels developed by the banks of the Loire for St Martin, Tours (see 28, page 77).

The chevet was adopted within 20 years for the

107 **Bernay** 1017–55, from the east.

Related in plan to Cluny II (see 21, page 66) but larger and
more elaborate in such details as the half columns applied to
the sides of the rectangular piers, Bernay introduces the
distinguished line of churches built both in Normandy and
England with lantern tower, triapsidal ends (later altered)
and three-storey elevations to nave and transepts – though
the gallery lacks depth, in the manner of a triforium.

cathedral of the ducal capital, Rouen, where it surrounded a sanctuary raised over a crypt. That, in turn, was the model for the abbey church of Notre-Dame that overawed the earlier St-Pierre at Jumièges, but there complex piers alternate with columns in the doubled bays of the nave.[108-109] Bernay's parallel apses and the alternating rhythm of Jumièges were imported into England by Edward the Confessor for his new abbey at Westminster, which was evidently meant to set the standard for replacing the inadequate stock of Anglo-Saxon cathedrals. Both were also retained in the second half of the century for the most prestigious of Norman works, the churches of Ste-Trinité and St-Etienne, Caen.[110-113] Built *ex voto* by William the Conqueror and his wife Matilda, these marked con-

108 **Jumièges, Notre-Dame** west front.

Like a Carolingian westwork, this is a powerful mass with superimposed spaces of its own rather than as an adjunct to nave and aisles. Its example was not forgotten in England, at Lincoln (1073), for example, or Winchester (see 114, page 247) – though the latter remained unrealised – but a much more integrated pair of towers already distinguished the abbey at Westminster (c. 1050–65) before the conquest.

109 PREVIOUS PAGES **Jumièges, Notre-Dame** 1037–67, ruins from the ambulatory.

Founded under ducal auspices, the plan followed soon after that of the cathedral begun before 1037 in Rouen, but the ambulatory lacked radiating chapels. There are piers with thin pilasters and attached columns to each face, those on the nave elevation rising through the gallery to support the diaphragm arches which carried the wooden roof, and shafts to each face alternate with columns in the manner popular with Norman builders in England. As we have seen, the alternation between column and rectangular pier was probably introduced to Ottonian Germany from Greece in the early 10th century, and imperial pretensions were certainly not foreign to Norman ducal patrons. The aisles were groin vaulted and the galleries above continued over the transepts (as often in Greece) and around the ambulatory. The Corinthianesque capitals are another possible connection with Germany and remote Greece.

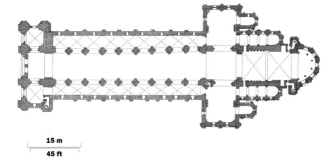

15 m
45 ft

110 **Caen, Abbaye-aux-Dames, Ste-Trinité** begun 1062, plan.

Built in emulation not only of Bernay (see 107, page 233) but also, more particularly, of Edward the Confessor's abbey at Westminster, the nave has the great length of its English predecessor, but the piers are uniform. There are five parallel apses at the east end, the main one with a free-standing arcade on two levels. Twin towers integrated with the main volume to the west were unfortunately reworked in the 19th century. Matilda was buried here in 1083.

siderable advance: the twin-towered west front was integral, the articulation of the internal elevations was rigorously logical, every element of the complex piers bearing a specific load in the almost-equally generous arcades of aisles and galleries, a wall passage throughout the clerestory level sustained visual depth, and the sanctuary of Ste-Trinité had a groin-vault.

When the Normans fulfilled the objective of effacing the essentially provincial Anglo-Saxon church with a metropolitan majesty matching their new royal status, the form of Bernay (see 107, page 233) – and the

111 **Caen, Abbaye-aux-Dames, Ste-Trinité** choir to the east.

The groin vaults may have been built for the burial of Matilda in 1083, groins were added soon after to the transepts, the nave had a wooden roof until c. 1115 or even later. The gallery throughout has the restricted dimensions of a triforium, but the clerestory has the depth of a considerable wall passage: the weight of the triforium and the depth of the clerestory are, of course, manifestations of the great mass represented by the multifaceted piers on which the Anglo-Norman church depends – structurally and aesthetically.

112 Caen, Abbaye-aux-Hommes, St-Etienne begun
c. 1068, nave to the west.

The east end was rebuilt in the early 13th century. The
grand nave survives from the original campaign of work.
The decorative triforium of Ste-Trinité cedes here to a
gallery arcade virtually matching the one below it in scale in
a scheme that approximated the degree of systemisation
achieved at Santiago de Compostela (see 102, page 218), but a
true triforium appears above the central crossing in the first
storey of the tower. Both aisles and galleries were vaulted –
with groins and quadrants respectively. The piers are
repeated with the slight variation of an added pilaster rising
to the string course below the clerestory between the paired
bays, possibly for aesthetic reasons, probably because
vaulting was envisaged from early in the building history.
From perhaps as early as 1115, the wooden roof was
replaced with ribbed groins over the doubled bays, and the
symmetry of the clerestory bays was distorted by the loss of
alternate side windows in each bay to accommodate the
intermediate ribs of a sexpartite scheme. The vaults of Ste-
Trinité, in contrast, are essentially quadripartite, but a
diaphragm arch inserted between the clerestory windows
divides the side zones into pairs of asymmetrical sub-bays.
The result has been termed 'pseudo-sexpartite'.

abbey at Westminster– persisted in plan but was transformed in elevation in emulation of Caen. Edward the Confessor's Westminster had ceded nothing in grandeur to its contemporaries in Normandy. Indeed, the grandeur of the Norman Romanesque developed in the series of abbeys and cathedrals begun in England under William the Conqueror – Battle Abbey near Hastings (1067), Canterbury and Bury (1070), Lincoln (1072), Old Sarum (1076), Rochester and St Albans (1077), Winchester (1079),[114] Worcester (1084), Gloucester (1087) – surpassed its model but was itself unsurpassed anywhere except at Cluny.

The dimensions were exceptionally grand, espe-

113 **Caen, Abbaye-aux-Hommes, St-Etienne** west front.

The westwork is no longer a self-contained entity: the towers, heightened in the 13th century, are integrated with the main mass of the building, though there are distinct chambers at the bases, and the central portico leads to a narthex unscreened from the nave. The disposition, especially with the original two-storey towers, persuasively recalls the ancient twin-towered palace portal (see volume 1, ORIGINS, page 84), ancestor of the Roman triumphal arch, threshold of apotheosis.

114 **Winchester, cathedral** begun 1079, model (Bayeux, Tapestry Museum).

In the first campaign of great church building under the Conqueror, affinity with Normandy was close, as Winchester demonstrates, though the Norman work survives only in the crypt and transepts, as the rest was rebuilt from 1189. The extreme length is English, though adopted in Ste-Trinité, Caen (see 110, page 239), and its steady increase may be traced from Canterbury (1070), via Lincoln (1072) and St Albans (1077), to its culmination at Winchester, asserting the conquest in the old Saxon capital with the longest building of its time – except for Cluny III (see 75, page 169).

Bishop Walkelyn, the patron and last Anglo-Saxon bishop of the see, 1070), retained the lantern of Bernay, the raised chancel and ambulatory of the cathedral at Rouen (dedicated 1063), but with orientated chapels like remote Corvey (see 26, page 75), he kept Ste-Trinité's clerestory passage and the grand gallery of St-Etienne, Caen (see 112, page 243), virtually repeating the scale of the aisle arcade as there but here subdivided with two interpolated arches, and he maintained the essentially Norman logical articulation of pilasters and half columns, each carrying a segment of the arcading or rising to provide visual support for the timber

ceiling. Foreign to Normandy, however, is the cushion-shaped capital popular in Germany. This had made its most prominent English appearance to date at Canterbury where the gallery of St-Etienne had also been introduced and the raised chancel of Rouen retained in a triapsidal sanctuary. In contrast and in direct competition nearby, the even longer abbey church of St Augustine, Canterbury (1073), reproduced the chevet.

cially the length of the nave, but monumentality was produced by the regular repetition of pure circular forms in precise masonry. Arcades were occasionally still supported by unarticulated rectangular blocks of Anglo-Saxon type, as at St Albans, and in the west, particularly, they were sometimes simply massive cylinders.[115] At their most Norman, as at Winchester, the great thick walls produced piers relieved with pilasters and semi-cylindrical shafts dividing the bays and supporting the intrados of arch within arch. The generous curves of those arches echoed from storey to storey, those of the gallery being subdivided internally into two, while the clerestories admitted ample light from triads through the depth of a wall passage. Unusually, there were three towers, though the original plan was for five.

In a second great campaign under the Conqueror's successors, planning was conservative, but the rigorous logic imported from Normandy for the first phase was relaxed and overlaid by a somewhat wayward approach to decoration, which has been identified as characteristically English. Inconsistency reigned. Noble simplicity might run to the prophetic elimination of the verticals altogether: this was anticipated

115 **Gloucester, cathedral** begun 1087, nave towards the choir.

The cylindrical piers that line the naves of Gloucester and the abbey at Tewkesbury (c. 1090) recall those of St-Philibert, Tournus (see 70, page 160) but, screening aisles two-thirds the height of the original Norman nave, they are far more massive. Over a reduced triforium, the clerestory was changed when the vault was inserted from 1242. It seems that the choirs of both buildings had galleries butting into the shafts of the great piers, producing putative four-storey elevations.

stupendously at Gloucester,[115] fully realised in the minster at Southwell[116] – where the three original towers survive – and was essential to the English Cistercian aesthetic in the context of the pointed arch.

On the other hand, there was much experimentation with varying the form of the pier and developing an alternating rhythm – anticipated at Notre-Dame, Jumièges (see 109, page 236–237) and Westminster, indeed in Ottonian Germany and Byzantine Greece – between rectangular piers with pilasters and half columns and cylindrical ones with or without attached shafts. The composite mode is generally more finely tuned, if not strictly logical anymore, and is represented nowhere better than by the cathedral at Peterborough where the purpose of the vertical shafts is clearly aesthetic – providing visual support for the wooden roof rather than the structure for missing groins.[117] The alternation of rectangular and cylindrical forms, the latter with a variety of essentially unarchitectonic spiral and chevron incisions, had reached its apogee earlier at the cathedral at Durham.[118-119]

Perhaps the major contribution of the Normans to medieval architecture was the development of the rib vault. A permutation of the form appeared in the tower

116 **Southwell** begun 1108, nave towards the crossing.

117 OVERLEAF **Peterborough** begun 1118, nave towards the sanctuary.

A monastery was founded on the site in 655, destroyed by the Danes in 870, refounded in 970 and destroyed by fire in 1116. The present church was consecrated in 1238 but Norman work has been replaced significantly only at the east end. Like Ely (begun 1083, nave mainly from 20 years later) and Norwich (begun 1096), the arches of the two main storeys have a third plane of arcading, each with roll

chambers of St Martin, Tours, as rebuilt c. 1050 (see 97, pages 210–211) and passed to Normandy with the rest of the legacy of that seminal work, appearing first in the chamber at the base of the north-west tower of the cathedral at Bayeux c. 1077. Doubtless in the knowledge of contemporary Lombard developments, probably brought by itinerant masons, ribs thereafter were applied consistently to the groin vault, though they were of stone rather than of brick, were more richly moulded and were set much higher than their earliest Italian counterparts. Their diagonals completed the articulation of the skeleton of arches upon which the high Romanesque church depends.

In Normandy the rib vault appears in the second decade of the 12th century at Lessay, in place of groin vaults originally projected at the beginning of

mouldings. The alternation of rectilinear and cylindrical piers distinguishes these works too, but the logic of Norman articulation cedes to English pragmatism: about the cylindrical piers individual support is denied to the inner recessions of the arches at the cathedral at Ely and the intermediate ones at Peterborough where, consequently, the ribs of the aisle vaults float free.

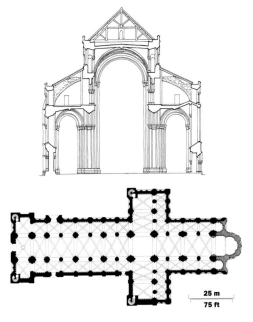

118 **Durham** begun 1093, transverse section and plan.

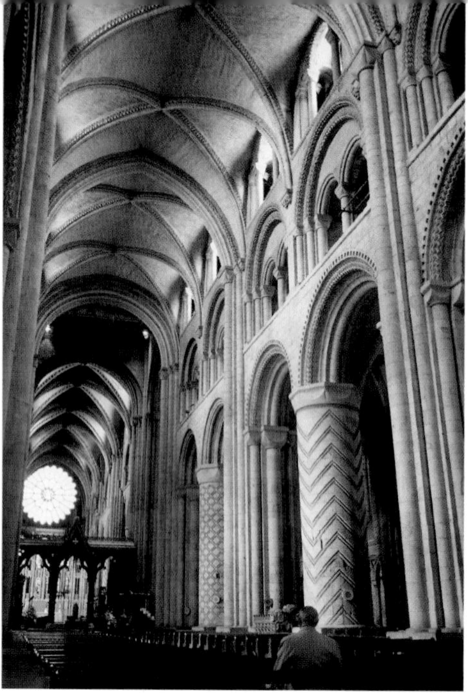

119 **Durham** nave towards the sanctuary.

The plan of Bernay (see 107, page 233) survived here until the ambulatory of the Chapel of the Nine Altars was added to the east end from 1242. The alternation of rectilinear and cylindrical piers of Ely is simplified by the elimination of shafts altogether from the latter, the arcading rising directly from their broad capitals, but complicated by the projection of much more assertive shafts between the paired bays. The aisles rise higher than those of the other major cathedrals of eastern England, if not as high as Gloucester or the abbey at Tewkesbury, and the gallery is reduced almost to a triforium: neither the grand gallery of St-Etienne nor Ste-Trinité's regular repetition of four shallow arches (see 111 and 112, pages 240 and 243), this consists of two pairs of arches framed by blind arcades carried in piers with attached columns, as at the abbey of Mont-St-Michel (began 1024) but here echoing the basic division of the main arcade into paired bays. The shafts of the cylindrical piers are incised with a bizarre variety of chevron and interlaced motifs in addition to oddly classical fluting.

There are two main planes to each of the arches, but they tend to coalesce into one rich form with a variety of profiles leading to a roll-moulding in the centre. The chevron motif in deep relief, rather than incised, plays a prominent part in

this context – as it did already in the new choir of
Canterbury built from the early 12th century on the double
transept scheme of Cluny III (see 69, page 158). And if a
structural member is overlaid with a non-structural one, as
the chevron on the column, the arch is reduced to the purely
decorative interlace along the side walls of the aisles. This
complete departure from Norman logic was to prove
particularly popular in England.

Vaulting was planned from the outset. Introduced
before 1099 over the sanctuary, defective construction led to
its replacement after the completion of the nave c. 1133.
The rib vaults were based on double bays as in the two great
churches of Caen, Ste-Trinité and St-Etienne, but they are
separated by pointed transverse arches supported by the
triads of boldly projecting shafts already noted and, rather
than sexpartite or pseudo-sexpartite, each section has seven
zones due to the elimination of the intermediate transverse
arch. The sexpartite system of St-Etienne was adopted in
early Gothic France, but the reintroduction of the transverse
arch to the system of Durham provided the key to the much
more rational quadripartite type of vaulting over single bays
that was universally adopted in the high Gothic period. In
England, as in Normandy, the earliest groin and rib vaults
were usually of rendered rubble.

the century, and at St-Etienne and Ste-Trinité, Caen in place of the original timber over the naves (see 111 and 112, pages 240 and 243). These all depend on doubled nave bays forming roughly square compartments divided by a diaphragm arch across the centre but, as semi-circular diagonals over squares will rise higher than the sides and the diaphragm, consistency of height could only be achieved by distorting the geometry or springing the arches from different heights (stilting). Both techniques were tried in these pioneering Norman works and found to be wanting, visually and structurally.

Much of this was anticipated at Durham, where the cathedral seems to have been designed for vaulting at the outset in 1093: the choir vault was completed by 1099, the choir c. 1104, the north transept a decade later and the nave vault by 1133. As at Caen, the system depends on doubled nave bays, but each section of the vault has seven compartments defined by a regular lattice of ribs. The use of pointed arches with semi-circular ones achieved consistent height in a way that was aesthetically and structurally far more satisfactory than stilting.

The pointed arch was prominent at Cluny III, but

in the context of the tunnel vault where its potential was only partially realised and the thrust of the tunnel was ultimately met with interpolated flying buttresses. Durham has quadrant arches hidden under the gallery roofs which anticipate these buttresses, but their primary role was probably to support the roofs rather than the clerestory wall. At Durham, however, the use of the rib vault with the pointed arch and the putative flying buttress marked the way ahead. In place of the thick walls and piers needed to meet the pressure of heavy tunnel vaults, the groin vault and its ribbed variety is carried at its corners and one buttresses another in a series – until the end where extraneous support is required. This realisation led to the revival of an antique structural principle admitting the free flow of space and light around slender pillars: the counter-opposition of forces in a fully integrated network of lateral and diagonal arches. Thus the rib in the tower of St Martin, Tours (see 97, pages 210–211) may be seen to have provided the key to an entirely new style: the Gothic, which was invented in the Ile-de-France within a decade of the completion of the vaulting at Durham.

The East

Meanwhile Norsemen had laid the foundations upon which the Russian empire was to be built. The Slav tribes, who emerged from the land between the Vistula and the Dnieper in the 1st century AD, slowly settled in European Russia, harried by the Huns, Avars and various Turkish tribes. Vikings, called Rus, offered themselves as allies and founded forts at Novgorod in the north, Kiev in the south. Trade – in fur, above all – was their chief interest and to develop it they extended protection over a steadily increasing area, leaving the tribesmen autonomous provided they acknowledged their suzerainty and paid tribute.

Oleg, prince of Kiev entered into a commercial treaty with Byzantium in the fateful year 911 – when Normandy was conceded to his distant cousins. The imperial power of Byzantium might wax and wane but the city of Constantine stood on its ancient Greek foundations at the crossroads of trade: east–west by sea to Italy and Spain or by the Danube to Central Europe, north–south across Russia to Scandinavia. To the barbarians of the north and east, with trade went Christianity and with Christianity went culture. In c. 860, two missionaries from Salonica, Cyril (d. 869) and Methodius, followed the traders in the Balkans and took Christianity – and an alphabet (the Cyrillic) – to the Slavs and Bulgars.[120]

Following the trade routes across Russia, Christianity also claimed the ruler of Kiev. Oleg's successors took Slav names and it was his great-grandson, Vladimir the Saint, who converted to the orthodox faith in 988. Novgorod followed and after Vladimir's death in 1015 rivalry among his sons was terminated by the triumph of its prince, Yaroslav (1019–54). He united all the Rus domains and took Kiev, which was recognised as a grand-duchy. The patriarch of Constantinople extended his authority over it in 1037, and the metropolitan who exercised that authority was

120 **Studenica, monastery with the Church of the Virgin** late 12th century.

Western Romanesque in its tunnel-vaulted, aisleless nave, specifically Italianate in its external articulation with pilasters and corbel-table frieze of blind arches, this work is also Byzantine in its dome and in the style of its magnificent frescos (see volume 4, IMPERIAL SPACE, page 124). Such cross-fertilisation of the two main strands of early medieval Christian architecture is natural to the border area between

the Catholic and Orthodox worlds. The Romanesque was imported into Dalmatia from Italy, but was arrested before penetrating much further into the Balkans than Studenica by the Byzantine style of the missionaries from Greece who succeeded, where the Latins had failed, in giving an alphabet to the southern Slavs. In the north, on the other hand, the Romanesque was exported with Catholicism from Germany to the central Slavs of north-central Europe and prevailed through Poland to the borders of the orthodox Russias.

glossary

ACANTHUS plant, stylised images of whose leaves are characteristic of CORINTHIAN CAPITALS.

ADDORSED back-to-back.

AEDICULE ornamental pilastered niche to house a sacred image, for example.

AISLE side passage of a church or temple, running parallel to the NAVE and separated from it by COLUMNS or PIERS.

ALCAZAR any of a series of palaces built by the Moors in Spain. From Arabic al QASR.

ALTAR focus of attention in religious ritual; the communion table in a Christian church.

AMBULATORY semi-circular or polygonal arcade or walkway.

APSE semi-circular domed or vaulted space, especially at one end of a BASILICA. Hence APSIDAL, in the shape of an apse.

AQUEDUCT artificial channel or conduit for water.

ARCADE series of arches supported by COLUMNS, sometimes paired and covered so as to form a walkway.

ARCH, DIAPHRAGM in which the area from springing line to apex is made blind with an infill.

ARCH, STILTED in which an interpolated PIER raises the springing line above the IMPOST.

ASHLAR masonry cut and placed in horizontal courses with vertical joints, so as to present a smooth surface.

ATRIUM entrance-hall or courtyard, often open to the sky.

AULA REGIA public audience chamber or throneroom in a royal or imperial court.

BAILEY courtyard protected by outer defensive wall. See also MOTTE AND BAILEY

BAPTISTRY building dedicated to the rite of baptism.

BASILICA temple or other public building, consisting principally of a COLONNADED rectangular space enclosed by an AMBULATORY or having a central NAVE and side AISLES, and generally lit by a CLERESTORY.

BASTION structure projecting from the angle of a defensive wall, enabling enhanced vision and mobility for a garrison.

BAY one of a series of compartments of the interior of a building, the divisions being created by PIERS or COLUMNS, for example.

BELFRY bell-tower or the particular room in a bell-tower where the bells are hung.

BUTTRESS support, usually stone, built against a wall to reinforce or take load.

CALIPH muslim religious and secular ruler, originally one of the companions of Muhammad. Hence CALIPHATE.

CAMPANILE bell-tower, usually freestanding.

CANOPY roof for a niche or statue, often supported by slender poles.

CANOPY VAULT see VAULT, CANOPY.

CAPITAL top part of a COLUMN, wider than the body of the SHAFT, usually formed and decorated more or less elaborately.

CHANCEL part of a church where the clergy and choir are ranged, separated by a screen or railing from the main body of the building.

CHAPEL subsidiary space having its own ALTAR, situated within a larger church or cathedral.

CHAPTER assembly of canons in a cathedral or abbot and senior monks in a monastery, responsible for managing institutional affairs.

CHAPTER HOUSE room or building within or adjacent to a monastery or cathedral, in which the CHAPTER meets.

CHEVRON decorative moulding composed of a zigzag pattern.

CHOIR area of a church near the ALTAR, in which the choir (singers) sit.

CITADEL fortress, usually at the highest part of a town.

CLERESTORY windowed upper level providing light for a double-storey interior.

CLOISTER covered ARCADE, often running around the perimeter of an open courtyard.

COLONNADE line of regularly spaced COLUMNS.

COLONNETTE small COLUMN, decorative and/or functional.

COLUMN vertical member, usually circular in cross-section, functionally structural or ornamental or both, comprising a base, SHAFT and CAPITAL.

CONCRETE building material composed of cement agglomerated with sand, gravel, stone chippings, et cetera.

CORBEL course of masonry or support bracket, usually stone, for a beam or other horizontal member. Hence corbelled, forming a stepped roof from progressively overlapping corbels.

CORINTHIAN ORDER *see* ORDER, CORINTHIAN.

CROSSING the area where the TRANSEPT of a church crosses the NAVE and CHANCEL, often surmounted by a tower.

CRYPT underground chamber, often beneath the CHANCEL of a church.

CUSP projection formed between two arcs, especially in stone tracery, hence CUSPED.

DADO the middle part, between base and cornice, of a pedestal or the lower part of a wall when treated as a continuous pedestal.

DIAPHRAGM ARCH *see* ARCH, DIAPHRAGM.

DOME more or less hemispherical roof or vault, hence DOMICAL.

EAVES the part of a roof which overhangs the outer face of a wall.

EN ECHELON disposed in parallel, like the rungs of a ladder. (See page 76.)

EXARCH senior bishop in the orthodox church, also provincial governor in the Byzantine empire: hence EXARCHATE.

FLUTING decorative vertical grooves incised on a COLUMN.

FLYING BUTTRESS an arch and more or less freestanding BUTTRESS which together take the load of a roof, for example.

FRESCO painting done on plaster which is not yet dry.

FRIEZE the middle part of an entablature, above the architrave and below the cornice, or more generally any horizontal strip decorated in RELIEF.

FRONTISPIECE principal entrance and its surround, usually distinguished by decoration and often standing proud of the façade in which it sits.

GABLE more or less triangular vertical area formed by the ends of the inclined planes of a pitched roof.

GALLERY upper storey projecting over the main space.

GOTHIC ARCHITECTURE style featuring pointed arches, RIB VAULTS and FLYING BUTTRESSES, which prevailed in Western Europe roughly from the 12th century to the 16th.

GROIN VAULT *see* VAULT, GROIN

ICON image of a sacred subject, often acquiring sacred significance in its own right. Hence ICONIC, possessing sacred significance.

ICONOCLASM movement within the 8th–9th century orthodox church, devoted to the destruction of ICONS; more generally a doctrine of questioning or undermining established beliefs.

IMPOST structural member – usually in the form of a MOULDING or block – at the top of a pillar, for example, on which an arch rests.

INTRADOS curve defined by the lower surface of an arch.

KEEP main tower of a castle, providing living accommodation.

LADY CHAPEL a CHAPEL dedicated to the Virgin Mary.

LANTERN TOWER windowed structure lighting an interior, situated on a roof, often at the apex of a DOME.

LINTEL horizontal member over a window or doorway, or bridging the gap between two COLUMNS or PIERS.

MINSTER cathedral or major church attached to a monastery.

MOSAIC decoration formed by embedding small coloured tiles or pieces of glass (TESSERAE) in cement.

MOSQUE muslim temple/complex: defining physical embodiment of muslim ideology.

MOTTE AND BAILEY defence structure composed of a steep mound (motte) usually surmounted by a tower, the whole being situated within a walled courtyard (bailey). (See page 220.)

MOULDING the contour of a projecting or inset element.

NARTHEX chamber adjunct to the NAVE of a public building, usually a Christian church.

NAVE central body of principal interior of, for instance, a church or temple.

NECROPOLIS cemetery, literally a community of the dead.

ORDER defining feature of classical architecture, comprising a COLUMN together with its entablature.

ORDER, CORINTHIAN characterised by an elaborate decorative arrangement of ACANTHUS leaveson the CAPITAL.

PALISADE defensive structure of wooden stakes driven into the ground.

PEDESTAL base supporting for example a COLUMN or statue.

PENDENTIVE curved concave triangular member used at the corners of a square or polygonal structure so as to enable reconciliation with a domed roof.

PIER supporting pillar for a wall or roof, often of rectangular cross-section.

PILASTER a PIER of rectangular cross-section, more or less integral with and only slightly projecting from the wall which it supports.

PORTA COELI gate of heaven.

PORTAL doorway, usually on the grand scale.

PRESBYTERY area reserved for clergy, at the eastern end of a church, in which the main ALTAR is situated.

QASR Arabic term for a castle.

QUATREFOIL having a curved shape composed of four subsidiary curves.

QUINCUNX structure composed of an agglomeration of five elements, four being identical and disposed to form more or less a hollow square, its centre being filled by the fifth.

QUOIN external corner of a building, where the stones thereof are arranged to form a key pattern. (See page 82.)

RELIEF carving, typically of figures, raised from a flat background usually by cutting away more (HIGH RELIEF) or less (LOW RELIEF) of the material from which they are carved.

RELIQUARY vessel or chamber holding relics of the saints, often in the form of bones or mummified bodyparts.

REVETMENT decorative reinforced facing for a retaining wall.

RIB raised band on a vault or ceiling.

RIB VAULT see VAULT, RIB.

ROLL MOULDING plain moulding with semi-circular cross-section.

ROMANESQUE ARCHITECTURE style featuring massive masonry constructions with groin vaults and round arches, which prevailed in Western Europe roughly from the 8th century to the 12th, when it was superseded by the GOTHIC.

ROOF, TRUSSED roof supported on one or more TRUSSES.

ROTUNDA circular room or building, usually with a domed roof.

SANCTUARY the most sacred part of a church or temple, often where the ALTAR is situated.

SARCOPHAGUS stone outer coffin, often highly decorated.

SEPULCHRE tomb.

SHAFT more or less cylindrical element of a COLUMN rising from the base to the CAPITAL.

SHRINE church or part thereof revered because of particular association with a saint or sacred object.

SPIRE elongated conical or pyramidal shape forming the apex of a tower.

SQUINCH arch placed across the corner of a square structure so as to form a polygon capable of being roofed by a dome.

STILTED ARCH see ARCH, STILTED.

STRING COURSE projecting horizontal course of structural elements or MOULDING.

TESSERA small tile made of marble or glass used to form MOSAIC.

TRANSEPT part of a large public/religious building that crosses the NAVE at right angles.

TREFOIL having a curved shape composed of three subsidiary curves.

TRIBUNE gallery of a church. (See page 49.)

TRIFORIUM arcaded corridor facing on to the NAVE or CHANCEL of a church, situated immediately below the CLERESTORY.

TRIUMPHAL ARCH monument commemorating a victory, often taking the form of a massive rectangle penetrated by an arch.

TRUSS timber or metal framework formed so as to support, for instance, a roof.

TRUSSED ROOF see ROOF, TRUSSED.

TURRET small tower, often at the angle of a building.

TYMPANUM an area, usually recessed, formed by a LINTEL below and an arch above.

VAULT structure forming an arched roof over a space.

VAULT, CANOPY creating a roof for a niche or tomb.

VAULT, GROIN enclosing a space composed of two intersecting, more or less hemicylindrical, shapes.

VAULT, RIB composed of load-bearing ribs, carrying the material which fills the spaces between them.

VAULT, TUNNEL enclosing a more or less hemicylindrical space.

VESTIBULE hallway to a building; space adjunct to a larger room.

VILLA freestanding house, originally Roman country house.

VOUSSOIR wedge-shaped stone deployed
in building an arch. Hence voussoir
arch where such stones are used.

WARD courtyard protected by the outer
walls of a castle.

WESTWORK entrance-hall and
superstructure at the west end of a
Romanesque or Carolingian church.
(See page 43.)

The books listed below are those the author found particularly
  useful as sources of information on the architecture covered in
  this volume.

Conant, Kenneth John, *Carolingian and Romanesque
  Architecture 800–1200 (The Pelican History of Art)*, revised
  edition, Harmondsworth 1974
Taylor, H M, and Taylor, Joan, *Anglo Saxon Architecture*,
  Cambridge 1965
Anderson, William, *Castles of Europe from Charlemagne to the
  Renaissance*, London 1970

bibliography

index

Figures in bold refer to the text; those in
  ordinary type refer to captions; and
  those in ordinary type with an asterisk
  refer to illustrations.

This 25-volume series tells the story of architecture from the earliest settlements in the Euphrates and Jordan valleys to the sophisticated buildings of the late twentieth century. Each volume sets the buildings described and illustrated within their political, social, cultural and technological contexts, exploring architecture not only as the development of form but as an expression of the civilisations within which it evolved. The series focuses on the classical tradition from its origins, through its seminal realisation in ancient Greece and Rome, to the Renaissance, neo-classicism, eclecticism, modernism and post-modernism, supplemented with excursions to India and south-east Asia.

CHRISTOPHER TADGELL taught architectural history at the Kent Institute of Art and Design and has lectured widely in Britain and the USA.

● ● ● **a history of architecture** christopher tadgell **11**

gothic cathedrals
light and emancipation

Around the middle of the twelfth century, the nature of the Christian church was transformed with the invention of a new style, later derided by Renaissance classicists as 'Gothic'. Whereas Romanesque architecture was dark and massive, Gothic was light both in terms of mass and in its goal of flooding spaces with light. The style evolved to match a theology of light – light as a manifestation of God's grace. Gothic architects developed virtuoso arrangments of columns and arches – in effect skeletons in which walls had no structural role. As the style matured, formerly load-transmitting elements became decoration, webs of ribs masking rather than elucidating structure.

This book describes the development of Gothic architecture in religious building, up to the point at which men looked back to the techniques of ancient Rome to solve the problems of vaulting huge spaces.